WHAT KEEPS US
CATHOLIC?

40 REASONS
to feel good about our faith

MIKE DALEY

**TWENTY-THIRD
PUBLICATIONS**
twentythirdpublications.com

TWENTY-THIRD PUBLICATIONS
One Montauk Avenue, Suite 200
New London, CT 06320
(860) 437-3012 or (800) 321-0411
www.twentythirdpublications.com

Cover photo: PATRICE THEBAULT/CIRIC

ISBN: 978-1-62785-354-5
Library of Congress Control Number: 2017960974
Printed in the U.S.A.

 A division of Bayard, Inc.

TABLE OF CONTENTS

ACKNOWLEDGMENTS

*I would like to thank
Eileen Connelly, OSU,
who first invited me
to give consideration
to the very question of the book,
and Trish Vanni and Dan Connors
for their editorial skills.*

1

INTRODUCTION

After several enthusiastic invites from a student's mother, I finally accepted her invitation to attend a large, nondenominational church with their family. This was a good "Catholic" family, mind you, with years of both local parish involvement and Catholic education. Yet not only had my student stopped practicing Catholicism, she and her family were now committed to this other faith community.

Talking with colleagues about the upcoming trip and the phenomenon of Protestant megachurches, our conversations were quick to describe these places as "theology lite" or "all entertainment, no substance." However, once I was there, I was impressed by the number of volunteers, and I felt a sense of community. These were people who, despite the size of the church, knew each other and were excited to be there. The free coffee didn't hurt either.

As the service began the pastor shared with the community something that he had never done before and something that he thought, given his personality, was next to impossible—he'd just been on a silent retreat. It was at a place several hours south, just outside Bardstown, Kentucky—the Abbey of Gethsemani. During his retreat, he was introduced to the thought and writings of Thomas Merton, the famous Trappist monk and the most noted American Catholic spiritual writer of the twentieth century. He asked the congregation, "Anybody ever heard of Thomas Merton?" At least half the hands went up.

As much as I wanted to believe that Thomas Merton's person and writings had transcended religious boundaries (which they have, given the continued popularity of his autobiography, *The Seven Storey Mountain*, and other books by or about him), I presumed that most of the people who raised their hands, like the family I had come with, were former Catholics. According to a survey published several years ago by the Pew Forum on Religion and Public Life, I had reason to believe this. The survey showed that approximately one-third of the respondents who were raised Catholic no longer describe themselves as Catholic. Across the general population this means that nearly ten percent of all American adults are former Catholics. Sadly, for me, this statistic includes my older brother.

As much as I want to blame my brother and the family who invited me to church with them for some defect on their part for no longer practicing Catholicism, in the end, I must honor their experience. The reasons they (and countless others) left are multiple and very convincing—lack of hospitality and community, irrelevant and uninspiring liturgies, disagreement over church teachings, need for a personal relationship with God, abuse and scandal, irregular marriages, and more.

All of this has led me to an important and essential question: What keeps *me* Catholic? And better yet, what keeps *us* Catholic?

Most of us, over our lifetimes, have been given enough reasons to leave, and yet we stay. We love the church. It's our home… warts and all.

In the reflections that follow, I invite you to join me in voicing the reasons as to "what keeps us Catholic." This book answers that question by focusing on our strengths. In the process, I hope, we can confirm our commitment to this imperfect but very beautiful tradition. I'm sure my reasons—community, saints, prayer, Mass, parish, school, word of God, humor, sacramentality, and many more—will be echoed by yours.

FOR FURTHER DISCUSSION AND REFLECTION

Who is someone that you know who no longer practices their Catholic faith? As difficult as it may be, have you been able to talk with them about their decision?

If asked for some words or phrases that describe Catholicism, what would you say?

2

GRATITUDE

I shouldn't complain, but I'm pretty good at it when I do. Especially about my family and childhood growing up. I'll spare you the details and offer the depressing highlights instead: frequent job changes, a heart-wrenching move on my tenth birthday, unemployment, divorce, bankruptcy, mental illness—not unlike many other families, I've come to find out.

Looking back on it all, though, rather than lamenting I'd rather focus on a gift that emerges among those hardships: my baptism into the Catholic tradition. Though my relationship with my parents has waned and withered, in this regard all I can say to them is, "Thank you." In good times and in bad, my Catholic faith has stayed with me all these years. Try as I may, I can't seem to get rid of it. In fact, through its graced worldview, being Catholic colors pretty much what I see, say, and do.

I remember when my oldest daughter celebrated her first reconciliation. Coming back to the pew, she had a relaxed smile on her face (I'm confident that all of her sins were venial ones). She drew near to me as I put my arm around her. After a few minutes, she looked at me encouragingly and said, "Daddy, I think you should go get in line." She quickly added, "I heard you and mommy fighting."

Though there were five priests available to hear confessions, I had my eyes set on only one. Approaching him, a sense of gratitude overwhelmed me. Memories flooded back…living next door to him at college…his witnessing our marriage and baptizing one of our kids…. I asked for forgiveness for my failings as a husband and a father. After absolution we held each other for a few moments, at the end of which I said, "Thank you for your presence in my life."

Hanging on the wall in my classroom is a saying that strikes me deeply. It is attributed to a medieval Dominican mystic, Meister Eckhart. It reads: "If the only prayer in life you say is 'Thank You,' that would suffice." In light of it, I have often wondered what words or prayers my wife, children, students, and colleagues hear me offer. Are they selfless or selfish? Sadly, I think I already know the answer.

I'd like to blame it on the -isms of materialism, consumerism, and individualism. Ringing constantly in our ears are the messages of "You don't have enough. Get some more," and "Do it your way or no way." We'd rather acquire possessions than acknowledge our gifts and emphasize our independence instead of admitting our need for others. Frustratingly, this leaves us in a constant state of dissatisfaction, always desiring more.

Jesuit John Kavanaugh once remarked that he thought that ingratitude, not disobedience, was the original sin. Adam and Eve had everything in the Garden. The snake's deception was that of convincing them that they needed more. Unfortunately, that ruse worked.

Catholics have the antidotes to this attitude and lifestyle, though. They're called the Eucharist and the sacrament of reconciliation. The word "Eucharist" itself means "thanksgiving." In and through this sacramental gift—the very body and blood of Jesus the Christ—we are invited to say two words: "thank you." These words are hard to say and even more difficult to put into practice, however, until we recognize that who we are and what we have is gift. The language of "You owe me" and "I earned it" is foreign to Jesus. This is not what we say to one another at the table of the Lord, but "take, receive, share."

Likewise, through the sacrament of reconciliation, we humbly recognize and open ourselves up to the experience of God's mercy. The greatest gift found in developing a sense of gratitude is also its greatest challenge. For with gratitude we discover a God who is first and foremost love—a God who in spite of our envy and pride, dare we say ingratitude, always gives us another chance.

FOR FURTHER DISCUSSION AND REFLECTION

Recall a time when you truly experienced your faith as gift.

Whom do you need to say "thank you" to?

How do the sacraments of Eucharist and reconciliation help you live a life of greater gratitude?

3

WOMEN RELIGIOUS

A while back, wanting some gifts for our kids after a week's vacation away from them, my wife and I wandered into a toy store. Perusing the aisles, my "Catholic" eyes quickly caught a lunch box prominently displayed on a shelf.

On the lid was a Sister in full habit. With requisite ruler in hand, she was standing watch over a young girl who was writing the line, "I am personally responsible for the sins of the world" on the chalkboard. I passed on the purchase.

Getting ready to check out, for sale at the cash register was the real showstopper—Nunzilla. When wound up, it spit sparks of fire and waddled like a penguin. Though limited in its portrayal of women religious, it pictured a prominent stereotype very well. Not only have Sisters long been a staple Halloween costume, but they also have entered the elite world of novelty items. No small feat!

Juxtaposed with these examples, however, is another (and I believe truer) image of women religious. Over the years, my school has had its annual retreat at the motherhouse of the

Congregation of Divine Providence in northern Kentucky. You may remember it was made famous by the movie *Rain Man* and Dustin Hoffman's and Tom Cruise's long walk down its driveway of towering oaks.

I'm not drawn to that natural, yet imposing, image as much as to the community's cemetery. It is located on a small embankment out back of the motherhouse. Fanning out from a statue of the crucified Christ in the center are row upon row of headstones—plain, sand-colored crosses. All that's on them is a name and date of death. They are simple, almost understated, testaments to a life of service, most of it unrecognized and little rewarded. The first one dates from May 23, 1892. In all, more than two hundred fifty of the Sisters are buried there.

It is, to say the least, an impressive sight—these holy women, this cloud of witnesses, who have preceded us in faith.

Seeing them, one is reminded of the foundational role that women religious have played in both America's and the church's history. Arriving in 1727, they found harassment, suspicion, even outright bigotry, in a country then fearful of all things Catholic.

Despite this, these "pioneering" women persevered and established a parochial school system that continues to educate hundreds of thousands of students annually. Likewise, their initial attempts to care for the sick and needy developed into the highly professional and esteemed Catholic health care system of today. In short, at a time when the larger culture, even the church, was saying that a woman's place was only in the home, women religious were demonstrating that the world was where they belonged.

Summarized briefly: they have been faithful—to their consciences, their vows, their communities, the Catholic church, and the gospel of Jesus the Christ. Sure, we can all offer a Sister or nun who meets the supposed popular culture caricature, but we also know better. With limited means yet unbounded in determination and devotion, they "faithed" the American Catholic church into being.

Though reduced in numbers today, women religious continue to extend their mission and values to the church and world as spiritual directors and chaplains, teachers and writers, social workers and hospital administrators, activists and missionaries, and still others. As one woman religious recently stated, looking at the past and current state of their life, "I come to praise this life, not bury it."

Count me as another one who is here to praise and celebrate this life.

FOR FURTHER DISCUSSION AND REFLECTION

How has your life been touched, directly or indirectly, by the ministry of women religious?

4

VATICAN II

It comes with the season. Summer is hot here. As the temperatures rise, people seek refuge in their homes. They close their windows and crank up their air conditioners. Thankfully, fall arrives. With it, people are finally able to open their windows again and enjoy the outdoors. No longer do they need to protect themselves from the scorching sun and blazing heat.

This "opening of windows" scenario is also a central image of the Second Vatican Council (1962–1965). When Pope Saint John XXIII announced that he was convening an ecumenical council, many people, having never experienced one, didn't know what to think.

Trying his best to explain what "aggiornamento" meant to a group of bishops, the pope sensed that his words about church renewal and responding to the "signs of the times" were falling on deaf ears. To better illustrate what "bringing up to date" entailed, Pope John went to the nearest window, opened it, and said, "The church needs to let in some fresh air."

The Catholic church gathered in council to look at who

it was, both internally and externally. Some saw only decay, destruction, and death. To this, John XXIII, who was canonized by Pope Francis in 2014, said, "We feel we must disagree with these prophets of gloom, who are always forecasting disaster, as though the end of the world were at hand." Rather than avoid the world as a den of iniquity, the Catholic church at the Second Vatican Council embraced it as a graced community, placing itself at the service of all of humanity, whom it sought to make more whole through Jesus the Christ.

This conciliar sentiment is most vividly expressed in the Pastoral Constitution on the Church in the Modern World (*Gaudium et Spes*). Its introduction, though written decades ago, still reads as if the ink is wet: "The joys and the hopes, the griefs and the anguish of the people of our time, especially those who are poor or afflicted, are the joys and hopes, the grief and anguish of the followers of Christ as well. Nothing that is genuinely human fails to find an echo in their hearts."

Born in 1968, I am a child and student of the Council. All of my religious formation has been done in its light. This includes, as Cardinal Avery Dulles noted, an openness to the modern world, the "reformability" of the church, renewed attention to Scripture, the practice of collegiality at all levels of the church, an appreciation of diversity within the church (unity, yes; uniformity, no), the active role of the laity, reaffirmation of religious liberty, desire for better ecumenical relations with non-Catholics and dialogue with other faiths, and working for a more just world.

I have a firm commitment to the reforms of the Council. I also recognize the need to appreciate what came before me in faith. *Ressourcement* (a return to the sources) and *aggiorna-*

mento (updating or renewal), two words that characterize the substance of Vatican II, aren't opposed to one another but complementary. In order to go forward, we must be mindful of the past. Likewise, if the past is to have any relevance, its spiritual wisdom must be integrated into the lived experienced of believers. As Pope John stressed, "We're not here to guard a museum, but to cultivate a flourishing garden of life."

Catholicism, then, is never "either/or"—letter or spirit, continuity or discontinuity, *ressourcement* or *aggiornamento*—but always "both/and." When balanced well, Catholicism is a living tradition. The Second Vatican Council helps the church to live now and into the future.

FOR FURTHER DISCUSSION AND REFLECTION

*As referenced by Cardinal Dulles, which of the themes
of Vatican II most resonates with your faith?*

*How does the church help you respond to
"the signs of the times" in service to the world?*

5

BAPTISMAL REMINDERS

It's a sight that fills every cradle Catholic with dread: walking into church for Mass and seeing that the first few pews are not only filled, but that nicely dressed people are seated in them. Trouble. As we look more closely, the culprit is spied—a baby. Infant baptism. Are you kidding me? Mass is going to be ten to fifteen minutes longer than usual now. But, as I've come to experience over the years, in addition to the extra demand of time, this is also what keeps me Catholic.

Some years ago, a community embraced me in faith and, with God, graced me through the waters of baptism. In a world hardened by sin, God's people said, "Follow us in discipleship. We will show you the way to Jesus." Then, like Jesus in the Jordan being baptized by John, I heard God say to me, "You are my beloved son with whom I am well pleased." Finally, as with all good Catholics, this sacred event was celebrated with a party.

Honestly, I don't remember any of it.

Baptisms at church let us live it all again, however. More importantly, they allow us to recommit and renew our faith in Jesus. Knowing that we can't make it on our own, those who preceded us in faith are invoked in the Litany of Saints— Mother Mary, Michael the Archangel, Joseph the Worker, Mary of Magdala, and the list goes on. Our response, and how could it not be, is "Pray for us." Baptism reminds us that we need help and offers the rich resource of the saints.

I'm especially struck by the baptismal promises or, better said, questions. Theologically illiterate as I was as an infant, my parents and godparents gave assent to them on my behalf. Now, when we hear them, the challenge of practicing the faith is placed on us.

> Do you renounce sin, so as to live in the freedom of the children of God?
>
> Do you reject the lure of evil, so that sin may have no mastery over you?
>
> Do you reject Satan, the author and prince of sin?
>
> Do you believe in God, the Father almighty, creator of heaven and earth?
>
> Do you believe in Jesus Christ, his only Son, our Lord, who was born of the Virgin Mary, suffered death and was buried, rose again from the dead, and is seated at the right hand of the Father?
>
> Do you believe in the Holy Spirit, the Holy Catholic Church, the communion of saints, the forgiveness of sins, the resurrection of the body, and life everlasting?

With the support of a faith community, we are encouraged, strengthened, and enabled, sinners that we are, to say, "I DO."

With people making power plays of all sorts, baptism also

reminds us that, in God's eyes, we are all equal. Through the grace of baptism, prejudices due to ethnicity, race, sex, age, orientation, and wealth are confronted with the person and ministry of Jesus of Nazareth. Here one discovers the fundamental dignity of the human person. Radically so.

Pope Francis, referring to the sacrament of baptism, recently and emphatically said:

> This tells us that no one is useless in the Church—no one is useless in the Church!—and should anyone chance to say, some one of you, "Go home with you, you are useless!" that is not true. No one is useless in the Church. We are all needed to build this temple. No one is secondary: "Ah, I am the most important one in the Church!" No! We are all equal in the eyes of God. But, one of you might say, "Mr. Pope, sir, you are not equal to us." But I am just like each of you. We are all equal. We are all brothers and sisters.

How our church and world need baptismal reminders.

FOR FURTHER DISCUSSION AND REFLECTION

What makes it so difficult to live out the baptismal promises? And, as Pope Francis says, to be persons of equality?

6

FOR THE HUMANITY

Even to the most casual observer, it's been easy to see that the church has been taking it pretty hard on the chin. Most of the blows, sadly, have been self-inflicted.

It's like we keep hearing the deafening echo in our ears of St. Paul's words to the Romans: "I do not understand my own actions. For I do not do what I want, but I do the very thing I hate….I can will what is right, but I cannot do it. For I do not do the good I want, but the evil I do not want is what I do" (7:15–19).

Theologically, the Catholic church is said to possess the fullness of salvation. Classically stated, the church has all the necessary means for its members to live a life of holiness—the sacraments, proper doctrine, and authentic teachers and guides of Christ in bishops and the pope. In actuality, as a faith community living out Jesus' message and person, we often are far from it. I'm not going to question the divine origin of the church in the person of Jesus, but it's beyond a doubt that he entrusted it to humans—ones who at times are very weak, flawed, fearful, fragile, and broken. A quick look at Jesus' twelve apostles confirms this. Judas betrayed him. Peter denied him. The rest fled and hid. Not the best of starts for an up-and-coming religious movement.

I remember speaking with the parent of a student of mine. In the course of our conversation, she told me that she and her husband had made a conscious decision to no longer practice Catholicism. Too much sin and hypocrisy, she said. With both humor and truth, all I could say in return was that the church will always provide plenty of examples for us to stop being Catholic. Yet I remain. It has everything to do with still being a work in progress—myself and the church.

If there's one thing I fear the most as a parent, it's being found out—when the façade of knowing what I'm doing unravels and is witnessed by numerous persons, especially my wife and three kids. But alas, parenthood has a way of making me look like an amateur.

I'm a little better at admitting my shortcomings as a teacher and a Christian. I always smile when, during class discussions, a student will give one of the reasons for not going to church. Who wants to hang out with a bunch of hypocrites? They put on a show for one hour on Sunday and then do whatever they want the rest of the week.

Though I don't tell them then and there, I am one of those Christian hypocrites. In response to the phrase, "You might be the only Bible some people read today," I'm embarrassed knowing that on some days my actions wouldn't even get someone to crack open the cover.

In fact, every year on class night, when parents come to school to meet their sons' teachers, one of the first things I tell them is that I'll teach their child the substance of Christianity far better than I'll live it. At the very least, it's truth in advertising. We never, personally or institutionally, reach the ideal.

Herein lies one of the reasons we remain Catholic. It lets us own the shadow, weak, dark, and sinful side of ourselves. We admit and claim the church in its hypocrisy and sin as well. Good company if you ask me. As we frequently need to remind ourselves, the church is a hospital for sinners, not a country club for saints.

FOR FURTHER DISCUSSION AND REFLECTION

Whether generally known or personally experienced, what expression of the church's sin and hypocrisy stands out to you?

7

HOPE AND PRAYER

It seems to happen every presidential election cycle. The build-up of this or that candidate, from whatever political party, takes on messianic dimensions. The rhetoric rises to such a fever pitch one can almost imagine that the Kingdom of God will soon be realized in all its earthly fullness.

Then reality sets in. Wednesday morning. Come to find out a president was elected, not a savior. Whether one's candidate was the winner or loser, past excitement and enthusiasm toward the political process quickly gives way to present and future cynicism and despair about the state of the world.

But, as Dorothy Day, the cofounder of the Catholic Worker movement, once said, "No one has the right to sit down and feel hopeless. There's too much work to do." How often we confuse the active, participatory, and dedicated theological virtue of hope—a deep and abiding trust in God's providence—with a passive, noninvolved, and irresponsible understanding of it.

Jesus was hopeful about the coming Kingdom of God. He actively sought to bring it forth. Likewise, as disciples, we are called to be hopeful cocreators with Jesus in constructing and building up the Kingdom of God.

An advocate on behalf of the poor and marginalized, Dorothy Day's life was hopefully devoted to the "un's": the unemployed, undocumented, unborn, uninsured, unfed, unprotected, unwanted, and unhealthy. She once said in an interview, "If your brother's hungry, you feed him. You don't meet him at the door and say, 'Go be thou filled.' You sit him down and feed him."

It's the same today. Whether we're watching television, reading the newspaper, talking with coworkers, or doing volunteer work, the voices of the destitute and forgotten cry out to us, "Help!" We're obligated to respond and get involved to the degree that our time and talents allow.

If the New Evangelization stressed by recent popes is about anything, it will find Catholics proclaiming the gospel not only in words, but as much, if not more, in deeds. In the process, the dynamism, relevance, and substance of the Christian faith will shine forth for all the world to see.

Unfortunately, however, the Kingdom of God's timeline often doesn't match our own one-year, one-month, or one-day plans. We demand overnight results. Tensions have to be resolved by the end of a mission trip. Actions lasting several hours need to overcome years of neglect and discrimination.

Yet this is simply not the case. Here we are consoled, though, by a prayer by the late Jesuit scientist Pierre Teilhard de Chardin entitled "Patient Trust." It reminds us that the Kingdom is unfolding not according to our timeframe, but God's.

Above all, trust in the slow work of God.
We are quite naturally impatient in everything
to reach the end without delay.
We should like to skip the intermediate stages.
We are impatient of being on the way to do
something unknown, something new.
And yet, it is the law of all progress that it is made
by passing through some stages of instability—
and that it may take a very long time.

FOR FURTHER DISCUSSION AND REFLECTION

*What visible sign of God's in-breaking kingdom
brings you hope in a world inclined to despair?*

How do you put hope into action?

8

FOOD AND MEALS

It happens once a month—Welcome Sunday.

With three independently minded kids, I am surprised that there are no, well, fewer, complaints when they're told to get ready for Mass. Likewise, I'm pleasantly surprised when upon leaving home they all have smiling—well, no, frowning, faces. For them, the appeal of the Mass is that afterwards, in the school cafeteria, people will gather there for a social. New faces can meet current ones; current ones can converse with the ones who seem to have been there their whole lives. The only words that my kids hear, though, are FREE DONUTS.

Like most kids, throw food into the equation, and they'll be there. Putting the proverbial carrot before the meeting, attendance will soar at the event if we say food will be provided.

It's much the same at the Daley household. Food and meals. Ultimately, it's what keeps us together. Work and activities stretch us very thin, at times almost to the breaking point. But at the kitchen table, through the partaking of "our daily bread," we meet each other face to face. Though we may have just been arguing with a brother, sister, or spouse, now we have to ask them—politely—to pass the butter or even thank them for preparing the meal itself. My wife is much better than I at privileging this encounter of substance and persons.

Sadly, due to the divorce over twenty-five years ago, when my family—my mom, dad, and brothers—comes to the table, it's broken. This has been true for some years now. The memories are painful, the conversation is superficial, and the silence is awkward. As a result food and meals are something we'd rather avoid.

Yet as difficult as they are, these meetings are also humanizing and, as a result, essential. The caricatures, prejudices, and biased views we have of one another are brought into a greater and more complete perspective when we're seated across the table from them. Second chances are possible. Old hurts are put in their proper context. Renewal of family—nuclear and extended—relationships doesn't seem so far-fetched.

Jesus knew well this transforming dynamic between people and food. As Scripture attests, it was central to his person and ministry, whether with one person or five thousand. To the point where some wanted to use his enjoyment of food and meals as a mark against him—"Look, he is a glutton and a drunkard" (Matthew 11:19). In the end, though, it isn't so much *what* he ate that challenges us as *whom* he ate with—"tax collectors and sinners."

A prominent story in which the theme of food and meal looms large involves two disciples on the road to Emmaus (Luke 24). The crucifixion had been debilitating to the faith of these followers. As they are talking and debating about all the things that had just occurred, Jesus joins them—"but their eyes were prevented from recognizing him." Ironically, they respond in disbelief at the person's current events deficit. In response to their limited understanding of him, Jesus calls them "foolish and slow of heart" and goes on to explain to them the fullness of Scripture.

Later, as it appeared that they would part ways, the two urged the "stranger" to stay and have dinner with them. Then, while at table, Jesus took the bread, said the blessing, broke it, and gave it to them. In the process their eyes were opened and they saw him as he truly was. A stranger was revealed as their savior. Whether eucharistic or familiar, sacred or common, sharing food and meals provides this opportunity for company, which prompts conversation, which enables connections to be made. Unfortunately, our fast food culture minimizes this possibility.

The power of food and meals, though, is such that the brokenness of faith can lead to the wholeness of relationship. This actually allows us to image the life that is to come as an eternal and heavenly banquet—donuts are optional.

FOR FURTHER DISCUSSION AND REFLECTION

What role does food play in the practice of your faith?
Do you talk about your faith in the preparing
and sharing of meals at home?

Do you live out your faith through acts of charity, such as
donating food to a food bank, working at a soup kitchen, or
delivering a meal to a sick neighbor? Do you experience the
Eucharist as a privileged encounter where Jesus "feeds" you?

9

LAUGHTER

A few years back, *L'Osservatore Romano*, the Vatican's semi-official newspaper, had a congratulatory article celebrating *The Simpsons'* twentieth anniversary. Yes, I mean the show with the beer-guzzling, nuclear plant working, incompetent, overweight, and vulgar resident of Springfield, Homer Simpson.

With the intriguing and intellectual title, "Aristotle's Virtues and Homer's Donut," the piece described the show as a "tender and irreverent, scandalous and ironic, boisterous and profound, philosophical—and sometimes even theological—nutty synthesis of pop culture and of the lukewarm and nihilistic American middle class." Then, in a line you could miss if you weren't paying attention, it said that without the show, "today many would not know how to laugh." I agree…wholeheartedly.

Though it's hard to pick just one, of all *The Simpsons* episodes I've watched none has been more meaningful and substantive and funnier than "The Father, the Son, and the Holy Guest Star." It is so good that if I were to ever be given the position of director of religious education at a parish (and this next statement could very well disqualify me from ever getting that job), I would make it mandatory viewing for those in the RCIA. For me it bridges what it meant, what it means, and what it should mean to be Catholic. You'll be hard-pressed to suppress your laughter.

Imagine that! The Vatican encouraging us to laugh…about religion!

But how else could one celebrate, on successive days, Mardi Gras and Ash Wednesday? The health benefits of laughter have long been touted; it relieves stress, increases life expectancy, and supports general wellness. Add humor to a religious tradition and it just can't lose.

If you don't believe me, take a visit to the University of Notre Dame. Once on campus ask to see the Word of Life mural. You might get some blank stares at first. Ask to see "Touchdown Jesus" and they'll know just where to take you. It's the same thing, though—a huge, 134-foot high and 68-foot wide exterior mural on the University's library. At its height are Jesus' outstretched arms symbolizing blessing, crucifixion, and resurrection. Facing south toward the north end zone of Notre Dame's football stadium, the mural soon began to be called "Touchdown Jesus." You didn't know Jesus was a referee, did you?

No one has combined religion, athletics, and humor better than Notre Dame. At the height of their rivalry with the University of Miami, an exasperated Miami chaplain said, "God doesn't care who wins a football game."

Then-Notre Dame coach Lou Holtz replied, "But his mother does." I'm sure Mary's still chuckling.

As seriously as they took their discipleship in Jesus, the saints, at least the ones I like the best, had a lighter side as well.

Take St. Lawrence, the fourth-century deacon martyred during a Roman persecution. In the midst of his torture on a gridiron, he is said to have cried out, "This side's done. Turn me over." He's not the patron saint of comedians, roasters, and butchers for nothing. When Pope Saint John XXIII was asked how many people work in the Vatican, he replied, "About half."

Saint Teresa of Ávila wasn't above a quip of the tongue, either. Thrown into the mud while riding in a carriage, she said, "Lord, why did you let this happen to me?" To which God responded: "That's how I treat all my friends." St. Teresa quickly retorted, "Then it's no wonder you have so few of them." If God has a sense of humor, surely the members of his church must as well.

Speaking at Castel Gandolfo, Pope Benedict, never one to be taken for a comedian, once remarked: "I'm not a man who constantly thinks up jokes. But I think it's very important to be able to see the funny side of life and its joyful dimension and not to take everything too tragically. I'd also say it's necessary for my ministry. A writer once said that angels can fly because they don't take themselves too seriously. Maybe we could also fly a bit if we didn't think we were so important."

Whether it's the foibles and mistakes of its members, mispronounced prayers, billboards out in front of churches, and more, Catholics have much to be thankful for. Chief among them are the multiple reasons to laugh and have such fun with our faith.

FOR FURTHER DISCUSSION AND REFLECTION

Whether in the past or present day, we know people who have laughed at the Catholic Church in a ridiculing or demeaning way. When have you laughed, in a way that celebrates faith, with the church?

10

INTELLECTUAL
TRADITION

Once, when I was visiting my brother in North Carolina, my niece came out of a farmer's market carrying some calypso beans. She generously offered them to her relatives, and we were struck by the various black and white patterns (very similar to *yin* and *yang*) on them.

"How'd they get that way?" my niece asked her mother. "God made them that way," was the reply. Playing the devil's advocate, I responded, "They evolved." To this, I was asked, "You don't believe that now do you, Mike?" "Yes, I do," I offered. "Well, it would take more than a weekend to speak to that," she said. "It would take billions and billions of years," I answered.

Though I didn't realize it at the time, the two of us were entering into the heart of the Catholic intellectual tradition. At the center of it is a most significant question: Are faith and reason (science) contradictory or complementary?

Given the plural and dynamic cultural context from which

it emerged, rather than build a wall around itself, the early Christian faith community began a conversation—a search for the truth—with the world. It's one that has continued for more than two thousand years. We read about it in learned books and classic works of literature; we see it expressed in works of art and buildings; we live it out in acts of devotion and justice. It is the "stuff" of our everyday lives.

As Pope Saint John Paul II said in the encyclical *Fides et Ratio* (Faith and Reason): "Faith and reason are like two wings on which the human spirit rises to the contemplation of truth; and God has placed in the human heart a desire to know the truth—in a word, to know himself—so that, by knowing and loving God, men and women may also come to the fullness of truth about themselves." Yes, we are a believing and, necessarily, a thinking tradition. At its best Catholicism says that you cannot have one without the other.

But this dialogue can be demanding work. At times, we'd like to be able to simply ask, "What does the Bible say?" or "What does the church tell us to do?" But the Catholic intellectual tradition moves beyond faith to seek its understanding. We look to the cumulative wisdom of the past in light of the emerging insights—scientific, economic, political, sexual, technological—of the present.

Perhaps no one has better evidenced this than the thirteenth-century Dominican theologian/philosopher Thomas Aquinas. Though a deeply committed Christian, he spent the better part of his life building upon the truths that he discovered in the works of Greek philosophers, especially Aristotle, and Jewish and Muslim authors. In the process he gave testimony to the hard-won realization that in the search for *logos*

(Greek for "reason") one discovers the Logos—the Incarnate Word of God in Jesus of Nazareth.

It must be admitted, however, that at times the church has feared, resisted, even denied, the truth. Not too long ago there existed an *Index of Forbidden Books*, which told Catholics what books they were not permitted to read. Over the years, though, as a faith community we have come to realize that the truth, wherever it is found, need not be feared. Questions need not be avoided, for wherever the truth resides one also discovers the Truth—the God of Jesus the Christ.

FOR FURTHER DISCUSSION AND REFLECTION

Have you ever experienced any confusion or tension involving a truth of faith and a belief of science? What was it concerning? Who or what helped you respond to it?

What is one example in your life where faith and reason are complementary?

THE RISK
OF HEAVEN

As I was driving home this past weekend from visiting my in-laws, the highway grew increasingly flat and monotonous. Even with the window down and radio on, I was starting to tire. What I needed was a caffeine boost to get me through the last hour and a half of the drive home. Instead I got something even better.

Right at the edge of a field, rising above the corn stalks, was a billboard that read: "If You Died Today Do You Know Where You'd Spend Eternity?" I have to admit it woke me up a bit. Several hundred feet down the road, I passed another one that said, in even starker terms, "Hell Is Real!"

In the midst of this hellfire haze, I was reminded of a sign I had recently driven by several weeks in a row. Posted outside a small Baptist church, it had the ambiguous warning (or invitation): Prepare to Meet thy God. The questions that have remained with me ever since are *Who's my God?* and *Where does God want to send me?*

If Christian art and literature are any indication, it looks like God is an angry judge who's set on condemning me to hell. Notable artistically is the "Last Judgment" painted by Michelangelo, found in the Sistine Chapel. Here the damned, as their loss of relationship with God would attest, are pictured as pathetic and depraved figures. Fictionally, Dante's *Divine Comedy* (the *Inferno*) introduced generations to the physical horrors of hell. Interestingly, in hell's innermost circle, Satan is encased in ice; alone and isolated, contracting into nonbeing.

I'm reminded of a story about a man who prayed to the Lord. He wanted to know what heaven and hell were like. "Come, I will show you hell," said the Lord. They entered a room with a huge pot of stew in the middle. Surrounding it were angry, desperate, and starving people. Each held a spoon that reached the pot, but each spoon had a handle so much longer than their own arm that it could not be used to get the stew into their own mouths. The frustration and suffering were terrible.

"Now I will show you heaven," the Lord said. Surprisingly, the other room was identical to the first—the pot of stew, the group of people, and the same long-handled spoons. But here everyone was happy and well-nourished. "I don't understand," said the man. "Why are they happy here when they were miserable in the other room? Everything's the same, isn't it?"

"Here they have learned to feed each other," the Lord replied.

In a world mired in fear, despair, and cynicism, the church invites us to risk heaven; to offer ourselves in vulnerable relationship to one another and God in this life in anticipation of the next. Yes, hell exists and it is eternal. But the more important truth of faith and one our tradition emphasizes is that heaven exists and is real. It too is eternal and the God of Jesus the Christ wants us there. The church says as much through the canonization process, whereby it declares that said person is in heaven experiencing the fullness of relationship with God. It has never definitively said the same thing about someone being in hell.

Experience tells us, however, that there is power in fear, judgment, and condemnation. Following the ministry of Jesus, though, at its best, the church extends compassion, forgiveness, and mercy. This is gospel. Salvifically, in this story, sin and hell are not the end, but grace and heaven.

Like the church, we know that fear can stop or start behavior, but only love—and risking heaven—can transform it.

FOR FURTHER DISCUSSION AND REFLECTION

Who are you risking heaven for? The person you are offering mercy to rather than condemnation?

How are you preparing to meet thy God…in heaven?

DANGEROUS PEOPLE

I remember when my son, Brendan, celebrated his First Communion. As the date approached you could see both the excitement and nervousness on his face. One day his sister surprised him and said, "You even get some pretty nice gifts."

I don't know what he expected, but he received some checks from the grandparents, a nice picture frame, and a cross for his dresser. From one of my friends, though, he was hoping for something even better—soldiers. Not the cheap, green, plastic kind, mind you, but the painted, metal ones. Instead he got a nice, "generic" book of saints.

Looking through it later, his disappointment turned to interest, however, as I introduced him to some "battle-ready saints"— Ignatius of Loyola, Miguel Pro, Thomas Becket, George the Dragonslayer, Joan of Arc, and Isaac Jogues. A "dangerous" group of people, indeed.

If there's ever been a parental saying that's sure to have kids rolling their eyes or shaking their heads, it must be "You're judged by the company you keep." Usually we say it not as a compliment but when we're worried about where they're going or who they're hanging out with. Yet when it comes to what keeps us Catholic (and why we want our kids to remain Catholic), I can think of no better phrase to put into practice.

In this celebrity-obsessed age, however, our thoughts often turn to sports heroes, movie and television figures, and musicians. In so many cases role models one day become rogue figures the next. This is why many people are cynical about their so-called role models. No one lives up to the ideal. Why bother following someone when you're going to be let down in the end?

The church, however, has a tried-and-true group—the saints. These include persons throughout the ages whose constant goal was authenticity, wholeness, integrity, and holiness. Their model was Jesus. I'm reminded of the oft-quoted line by G.K. Chesterton: "It's not that Christianity was tried and found wanting. It's that it's never been tried." To this the saints reply, "We did it. It worked."

At the same time, it is reassuring (and maybe even a little surprising) to see that the church doesn't hide the faults and flaws of these role models of faith. St. Peter denied Jesus. St. Augustine was a sex-crazed young man. Dorothy Day, someone on the way to sainthood, had an abortion when she was younger. Saints were, first and foremost, human. Yet at some point in their lives, they were consumed with the desire to follow Christ more fully.

You don't have to be like them, though. As the great spiritual writer and Catholic monk Thomas Merton once said, "For me to be a saint means to be myself. Therefore the problem of sanctity and salvation is in fact the problem of finding out who I am and discovering my true self."

All of us know that information and books are important, but words only go so far. If we truly want to impart a lasting message, we always introduce our daughters and sons, students and godchildren to a person—someone whose life is worthy of imitation, someone who puts their words, and the person of Jesus, into action.

FOR FURTHER DISCUSSION AND REFLECTION

Which "dangerous person's" company do you keep?

In your path to being a saint, in the words of Merton, are you finding out and discovering your true self or hiding and running from it?

13

MARY

It was the closing hymn. Fittingly, since it was the feast of the Assumption, the selection was "Sing of Mary, Pure and Lowly." Turning the pages to that song, I was stopped in my tracks. Someone had written in the hymnal.

I was at a loss for words. What should I do? Looking at some of the other books nearby I didn't think it was a case of a serial Marian marker. I wasn't going to tell the pastor about this isolated incident. I thought of saying something to the music director, but then he might have thought I was just covering my tracks.

I looked again more closely at what had been done on the page. Someone had marked out the word "lowly" and replaced it with the word "humble." They'd also added "impoverished" to the song title. Thinking about it further, though not encouraging this type of behavior, I actually liked the title of this "new" Marian hymn better than the old one.

That incident paralleled a conversation that I'd recently had with a colleague. Asking him what came to mind when he thought of Mary, he responded, "The color blue. Not much else."

Returning the favor he asked me, "How about you?" I replied, "A statue. Usually with a crown on its head. The hands are clasped in prayer. Often a rosary hangs from them."

Unfortunately, many Catholics today tend to see Mary as someone outside of their historical experience, more as a picture of art than a person who truly lived, more as a hymn to sing than a human to relate to. As a result, appreciating Mary's significance for our faith and its practice is lost.

Mary is far too rich a resource of faith to let this happen. To do this, though, Mary must be taken off her pedestal. With her feet firmly on the ground, one discovers that her name, like Moses' sister of old, is Miriam. The religious tradition she faithfully practices is Judaism. The classic Catholic Marian doctrines of the Immaculate Conception and the Assumption are foreign to her ears.

More to the point, as a woman living in first-century Palestine, Miriam is struggling to survive a life marked by oppression. Economically she belongs to a peasant class that works the land with little compensation. Furthermore, given the people's taxes to Rome, Herod the Great, and temple, it is quite burdensome.

Politically, though, she retains the dangerous memory of the liberating story of Exodus; her homeland is occupied by a foreign power that cares little for the inhabitants and maintains control through violence. This will be illustrated most visibly in the death of her son by crucifixion.

Socially, as a woman, she is marginalized in a culture that privileges males. Strangely enough it is to this woman that the angel Gabriel appears, inviting her to partner with God in bringing forth the incarnation. With words that would alarm if only we took them seriously, Miriam joyfully sings:

> My soul proclaims the greatness of the Lord….
> He has shown might with his arm,
> Dispersed the arrogant of mind and heart.
> He has thrown down the rulers from their thrones,
> But lifted up the lowly…

As will soon be realized in her journey to Bethlehem, later escape to Egypt, and continued response to God's will in her life, rather than a plaster saint, Miriam emerges as a prophet and advocate of the poor. The woman who emerges is one who is both appealing as a model of faith, yet challenging in her exercise of discipleship.

This is the Miriam I've asked to introduce me to her son, Jesus.

FOR FURTHER DISCUSSION AND REFLECTION

How does your view of her change when Mary is rooted in her historical context?

Sit quietly with the Magnificat (Luke 1:46–55). What image of Mary emerges from it?

14

INTERRELIGIOUS
DIALOGUE

I don't often quote Latin, but if you say this phrase loud enough, you can either scare someone out of hell, condemn them to it, or make them think you're saying a spell from Harry Potter—"*Extra ecclesiam nulla salus*" ("Outside the church there is no salvation").

This is, of course, the classic Catholic phrase that was oft uttered when speaking of non-Catholics and non-Christians. As a result, Orthodox Christians were deemed "schismatics," while Protestants were termed "heretics."

Jews were in a class unto themselves, however. They were called "perfidious"—deliberately faithless, treacherous, and deceitful. In fact, the old Good Friday prayer for Jews offered "that Almighty God may remove the veil from their hearts, so that they, too, may acknowledge Jesus Christ our Lord." Blind to this truth, Jews had to be delivered from their darkness. Tragically, history is full of far too many examples of how

Christians have "delivered" Jews from their supposed lack of faith, including pogroms and other murderous acts.

This way of thinking was easy to live out when our interactions with Jews and other world religious traditions were limited. The religious and ethnic bubbles that used to shape us, however, no longer remain.

In ways almost unimaginable a generation ago, diversity and plurality surround us on a variety of levels—language, food, dress, and, most important, religion. What used to be a world away is now across the office, down the street, or a computer click away from us.

For Catholics, this reality was perhaps seen most concretely in Pope Saint John Paul II's visit to Assisi in 1986. There he held a historic interfaith gathering for world peace. In words that shouldn't surprise us, he said, "With the world religions we share a common respect of and obedience to conscience, which teaches all of us to seek the truth, to love and serve all individuals and people, and therefore to make peace among the nations."

As one noted theologian has long observed, though, there will be no peace among nations until there is peace among religions. This peace can only be achieved through dialogue.

This encouragement to enter into dialogue with other world religious traditions isn't something new for Catholics. At the Second Vatican Council (1962-1965), in the "Document on the Relationship of the Church to Non-Christian Religions" (*Nostra Aetate*), the Council fathers urged all Catholics "to enter with prudence and charity into discussion and collaboration with members of other religions."

Furthermore, the document said, "the Catholic Church rejects nothing of what is true and holy in these religions."

Not only does the Catholic church promote a level of basic literacy of its own beliefs and practices, it promotes this concerning other religious traditions as well. Having taught a world religions course over the years, it has been my experience that while learning about other religious traditions, the students also learned more about their own.

Through dialogue—engaged, participatory, reflective, two-way conversations—the church has come to realize that "Those who, through no fault of their own, do not know the Gospel of Christ or his church, but who nevertheless seek God with a sincere heart, and, moved by grace, try in their actions to do his will as they know it through the dictates of conscience—these too may attain salvation" (Dogmatic Constitution on the Church, 16).

In the process, then, though always proclaiming Jesus "as the way, truth, and life," Catholics are discovering in the words of St. Augustine "that the church has many that God has not; God has many that the church has not." So, rather than say "Outside the church," perhaps it's more correct to say "Without the church there is no salvation."

FOR FURTHER DISCUSSION AND REFLECTION

Whom do you know that belongs to another world religion— Judaism, Islam, Hinduism, Buddhism? How have they shared their faith with you? What do you know about their faith tradition?

Given that Jesus was a Jew, spend some time exploring and reading about the Jewish tradition.

15

SURPRISE

Though I'm having a hard time admitting it to myself, I'm now what's considered to be middle-aged. As much as I want to deny it, one thing that confirms this stage in my life at present is my dislike, even fear, of surprises.

To avoid them I usually arrive five minutes early for meetings, back up computer files, do preventive maintenance on our family cars and home, read the small print, eat and drink in moderation, put on sunblock, and save for the kids' college fund and my retirement. I want to be prepared…for whatever comes.

One of the reasons that many people are members of the Catholic church is because of the sense of stability and security it provides. There are rules to live by, authorities to provide guidance, access to God through the sacraments, and a community for support. When other aspects of life seem to fail, the one sure thing is Catholicism. No surprises please.

Yet a word many people have used these past few years describing the Catholic tradition is "surprise."

It began with the surprise announcement of Pope Benedict XVI's resignation (2013), when he admitted that he didn't have the strength of mind and body to continue. In the process he became the first pope in nearly six hundred years to step down from the office of the papacy.

At the conclave to elect the new pope there was an honest, but surprising, public recognition from numerous cardinal electors that the Vatican was in need of reform in terms of greater transparency, accountability, and efficiency. Though a program of change had been envisioned, no real clear candidate emerged.

When the white smoke cleared, and following the words *"Habemus papem,"* the church received an even greater, unexpected surprise—it was Jorge Bergoglio, the Cardinal Archbishop of Buenos Aires, Argentina, who was elected pope.

When all the excitement died down from that pronouncement, the surprises only continued. It was quickly pointed out that, although he has about as Italian a last name as you can get, he is the first pope from Latin America. Francis is also the first Jesuit to ever become pope.

Perhaps the greatest initial surprise, which I think no one saw coming, is his name—Francis. In explaining why he chose it, Pope Francis said that as votes appeared to be mounting in his favor, a cardinal friend said to him, "Don't forget the poor." "And those words came to me: the poor, the poor," Francis explained. "Then, right away, thinking of the poor, I thought of Francis of Assisi....How I would like a Church which is poor and for the poor!"

In the meantime, Pope Francis has declined the use of the papal apartment, preferring to live in a simple room at the

Casa Santa Marta where he stayed before he was elected. On his first (and now successive) Holy Thursday, at a juvenile detention center in Rome, he washed the feet of both women and non-Christians, which some suggested broke liturgical norms.

During his Easter Vigil homily, Pope Francis captured well the excitement, nervousness, and anxiety of his first few months: "Newness often makes us fearful, including the newness which God brings, the newness which God asks of us... often we would prefer to hold onto our security, to stand in front of a tomb, to think about someone who has died, someone who ultimately lives on only as a memory....We are afraid of God's surprises; we are afraid of God's surprises! He always surprises us!"

Easter is the liturgical season of surprise. What keeps us Catholic is the need for *surprise*. We are followers of a crucified person who was raised from the dead, brought to new life through resurrection, and now invites us into relationship with him. Surprise indeed.

FOR FURTHER DISCUSSION AND REFLECTION

In what positive and uplifting ways do you continue to be surprised by the Catholic tradition?

16

TRUST

Psychology 101. Trust is everything.

This truth is foundational to psychologist Erik Erikson's theory of how persons develop with respect to their interactions with family, friends, school, work, neighborhood, and nation. In their early years, if all goes well, building upon a parent's nurturing love and reliable presence, a child will respond to the world with trust, confidence, and a sense of well-being.

Recent public opinion polls would suggest, however, that things are not well with a variety of institutions and professions. A significant trust deficit appears to exist. Believing it tainted by political ideology or corrupted by corporate sponsors, Americans appear to have little faith in science. When it comes to rating the honesty and ethics of professions, trust in clergy and politicians has reached record lows. Whether considering the present or imagining the near future, it shouldn't surprise us that many Americans have little confidence in one another, as well.

A figure who allows us to rise above the increasing anxiety, doubt, despair, indeed mistrust, of the times is the English mystic Julian of Norwich (ca. 1342–1416). (We don't know her real name. She is called Julian because she lived and prayed at the church of St. Julian.) Julian's world was not unlike ours today, maybe even worse. Besetting her life and times were a number of political, health, economic, and spiritual crises: the Hundred Years War between England and France, the Black Death pandemic, peasant uprisings, and the religious turmoil brought on by the Avignon papacy followed by the Great Western Schism.

Julian easily could have been led to believe that she was living during the end times. All the signs were there. You could almost see the Four Horsemen of the Apocalypse—Conquest, War, Famine, and Death—on the horizon. While others, filled with the fear of damnation, were becoming overwhelmed by God's supposed wrath due to sin, Julian experienced and shared the assurance of God's love.

Simply put, Julian trusted in God's promise, goodness, compassion, mercy, and grace. It allowed her—rather than be limited by negativity, fear, insecurity and close-mindedness—to say confidently:

> All shall be well,
> And all shall be well,
> And all manner of things shall be well.

Likewise, as Pope Francis has so stressed,

> This "compassion" is the love of God for [humanity], it is
> mercy, i.e., the attitude of God in contact with human misery,
> with our poverty, our suffering, our anguish. The biblical term

"compassion" recalls the maternal viscera: a mother, in fact, experiences a reaction all her own, to the pain of her children. In this way does God love us, the Scripture says. And what is the fruit of this love? It is life!

Without trust, the life of faith is impossible.

The Catholic tradition stands upon Mary's trust in God's will. To the invitation to bring forth the Christ child, she responded, "Behold, I am the handmaid of the Lord. May it be done to me according to your word." That's why we call it Mary's *Fiat*, not *Caveat*.

Fear didn't hold Joseph and Mary back. Trust allowed them to be vulnerable to God's presence. Their son, Jesus, in the face of tremendous pain and suffering, uttered the words we long to be able to voice: "My Father, if it is possible, let this cup pass from me; yet, not as I will, but as you will."

Trust. It's what we long to be able to do. It's what we were made to do. Our models in faith tell us it's worth the risk.

FOR FURTHER DISCUSSION AND REFLECTION

*When have you said, like Mary and Jesus,
"not my will, God, but yours"?*

Who is someone you know that models well trust in God?

17

PROSPERITY, I MEAN DISCIPLESHIP

Against my better judgment, I bought a lottery ticket. Yes, I know the odds are statistically not in my favor but…I did it to support education in my state. And possibly win over three hundred fifty million dollars!

Prior to purchasing it, I had a little prayer pep talk with God. I explained that I had earmarked well over half my winnings to charitable causes. Of course, the church was a chief beneficiary. How could God refuse? Alas, it wasn't to be. Back to work on Monday.

Now, I don't mind when the state presents a money making scheme to me in the form of a lottery. I know what I'm getting into. When televangelists do it, however, it's a different story.

Taking a break from raking leaves, I turned on the television hoping to catch a quick update on some football scores. Instead, as I flipped through the channels, I got something even better—a Praise-a-Thon.

With energy and assurance in his voice, the preacher excitedly proclaimed, "I feel it. Right now. There's an anointing. Take a step of faith. Sow a seed and obey him. Because when the ground's wet that's when you sow." I smiled wryly and held onto a healthy dose of skepticism. The preacher went on: "It's not what I say, it's what God said. Poverty is spiritual; prosperity is spiritual. God's promise to you is prosperity; it's divine. Do it for Jesus, the Master. Precious saints, the anointing of God is flowing. I want to pray for those who need to prosper. I don't want to lose this anointing. Donate now. If the lines are locked down, go to the internet. Keep calling. God bless you. Don't hesitate; don't wait."

Oh, how we want to believe. For those who need a gentle nudge, there seems to be some scriptural merit to this so-called prosperity gospel—the fusion of financial success and physical health with the will of God. An oft-quoted verse is "The Lord will generously increase the fruit of your womb, the offspring of your livestock, and the produce of your soil, upon the land which the Lord swore to your ancestors he would give you. The Lord will open up for you his rich storehouse, the heavens, to give your land rain in due season and to bless all the works of your hands. You will lend to many nations but borrow from none" (Deuteronomy 28:11–12).

We could sure use the help. Mortgage payments. Car repairs. Credit card debt. School tuition. Yes. A new car. Vacation home. Financial invulnerability. Oops. I was getting a little carried away there.

That is the temptation of the prosperity gospel: to confuse wealth (what I have or want) with discipleship (whom I'm in relationship with—Jesus). To equate one's standing in the world with one's worth before God. To collapse life in this world with life in the one to come.

If anyone should have experienced material prosperity it should have been Jesus. Yet his life is a marked contrast to it. For Christians, even when it frightens us and we don't want to admit it, the great antidote to the delusion of the prosperity gospel is the cross. This symbol and the person on it are at the heart of our Catholic faith. The cross reminds us that in the end, however important wealth and health are, the only thing that we take with us into the next life is our relationship with God.

Being faithful to the gospel—the word of God—cost Jesus riches, societal privilege, and his earthly life. Pain and suffering were not minimized but magnified. Now Jesus didn't ask for this as some sort of perverse pleasure. It was the cost of discipleship.

In this regard, I've long been challenged by a quote attributed to Mother Teresa: "God doesn't call us to be successful, he calls us to be faithful." Living in a world that easily distracts, confuses, misleads, and tempts us to believe that prosperity is our vocation, Jesus' gospel calls us to faithful discipleship—a living out of his life and person.

FOR FURTHER DISCUSSION AND REFLECTION

Has wealth or the desire for it ever been an obstacle to greater discipleship with Jesus?

Like Mother Teresa, how are you being called to greater faithfulness?

18

THE ENVIRONMENT
AND SR. DOROTHY STANG

They called her the "Angel of the Amazon." For close to forty years Sister Dorothy lived in Brazil fighting for two things: 1) the poor, peasant farmers who daily are being exploited and manipulated by loggers, miners, and ranchers; and 2) the tropical rainforest, which, due to development by multinational corporations and ravaging by bulldozers, faces significant and possibly irreversible destruction.

Sr. Dorothy literally wore these commitments on her person. One of her favorite and often worn T-shirts read: "The death of the forest is the end of our lives." In response to the various threats to life that surrounded her, over the years she developed sustainable agricultural programs that provided jobs and food for the indigenous people, opened schools for education, and established health clinics.

Her work on behalf of justice should not be surprising as Sister Dorothy was a member of the Sisters of Notre Dame de Namur. Their mission: "make known God's goodness and love of the poor through a Gospel way of life, community and prayer. Continuing a strong educational tradition, we take our stand with poor people, especially women and children, in the most abandoned places. Each of us commits her one and only life to work with others to create justice and peace for all."

Though tragic, given who she was and what she did, it was not unexpected that seventy-three-year-old Sister Dorothy was martyred for her beliefs. In 2005, on a rain-soaked Saturday, she was traveling to a village along a muddy jungle road. She was approached by two gunmen hired by a local landowner. They asked her if she was carrying any weapon. She responded by reaching into her bag, pulling out her Bible, and reputedly saying, "This is my only weapon." She then began reciting the Beatitudes. "Blessed are the poor in spirit, for theirs is the kingdom of God. Blessed are those who mourn…." When Sister Dorothy finished reading them, she closed her Bible and began walking away. It was at this point that the gunmen fired six shots at point-blank range, killing her.

Some wrote her off as a tree-hugging, granola-eating, and sandal-wearing activist who got what she deserved meddling in issues and places where she didn't belong. But, like Sister Dorothy, noted voices in the church have urged greater environmental awareness and action. In their pastoral statement *Renewing the Earth*, the United States bishops highlighted the reality that, "Today, humanity is at a crossroads. Having read the signs of the times, we can either ignore the harm we see and witness further damage, or we can take up our responsibilities to the Creator and creation with renewed courage and commitment."

This quote leads us either to the culmination or perversion of Scripture's words that emphasize the gift of and care for creation. Interestingly and sacramentally, the ministry of Jesus and his gospel message are filled with the language of the natural environment. With polluted air, contaminated water, and toxic soil, the very substance of our sacramental vision, which sees humanity as encountering God through creation, is imperiled.

Pope Francis reminds us that "God always forgives, but the earth does not." More positively, in *Laudato Si'*, his encyclical on the environment, he states: "The entire material universe speaks of God's love, his boundless affection for us. Soil, water, mountains: everything is, as it were, a caress of God."

This leaves us with a challenge Pope Benedict raised in his encyclical *Charity in Truth*: "The way humanity treats the environment influences the way it treats itself, and vice versa. This invites contemporary society to a serious review of its life-style...."

Through the words and actions of Jesus, St. Francis, Popes Benedict and Francis, and Sr. Dorothy Stang, we are called as Catholics to a far greater environmental consciousness.

FOR FURTHER DISCUSSION AND REFLECTION

What are you doing, whether at home, through your parish, or in the wider community, to care for the earth?

How do you experience the presence of God in and through nature?

19

INSTABILITY

As I pulled up to the red light, I saw the arm hanging outside the window, cigarette in hand. Cautiously, not wanting to make eye contact, I looked things over. The pickup had seen better days. No rims on the wheels and rusting throughout the body. Junk and trash were littered in the truck bed. Then, nervously, I spied a glance at him. "Scruffy" is probably the best word I can use to describe what he looked like. What really caught my attention though was his tattoo. Visibly, on his forearm, were letters. I spelled them out— U-N-S-T-A-B-L-E. I was a little taken a back—UNSTABLE. At least I'd been warned.

Now I don't often picture Jesus in a pickup truck, smoking a cigarette, with a tattoo on his arm, but…you never know. As the encounter continues to fade from memory, the word "unstable" hasn't. If Jesus' person and ministry were characterized by anything it was instability.

We get a hint of this "imbalancing act" and what's to come later in Jesus' life in Mary's Magnificat (Luke 1:46, 51–53): "My soul proclaims the greatness of the Lord....He has shown might with his arm, dispersed the arrogant of mind and heart. He has thrown down the rulers from their thrones but lifted up the lowly. The hungry he has filled with good things; the rich he has sent away empty." Is it any wonder that there eventually will be a price on Jesus' head? Who really wants to live in a world where the first are last and the last are first? That's too much instability.

Rather than be embraced by his hometown of Nazareth for bringing glad tidings to the poor, liberty to captives, recovery of sight to the blind, and freedom to the oppressed, the townspeople were infuriated at this upstart preacher, especially his comparisons to the prophets Elijah and Elisha (Luke 4:16–30). Jesus challenged their expectations as to who and what a messiah was then and still for us today. Ask St. Peter (Matthew 16:13–28).

Just when we're ready to settle into our routines and relax knowing what's coming next, Jesus upsets things all over again with his words. We're told to love our enemies and to pray for those who persecute us. He tells us that we cannot serve both God and mammon. Then there's the supposed blessedness of the Beatitudes. Another hard one is to stop judging others. Doesn't Jesus know the type of people we work with?

It's like he wants to rob us of our complacency of faith or something.

Pope Francis has made some people nervous and unstable as well. Upon becoming pope, in an interview for Jesuit publications, he called the church to be more inclusive saying: "This church with which we should be thinking is the home of all, not a small chapel that can hold only a small group of selected people. We must not reduce the bosom of the universal church to a nest protecting our mediocrity." He went on to admit that the church at times "has locked itself up in small things, in small-minded rules" going so far as to say that "we have to find a new balance; otherwise even the moral edifice of the church is likely to fall like a house of cards, losing the freshness and fragrance of the Gospel."

Though the first impulse may be to seek safety and security, Jesus is just as likely to be found in the margins, shadows, alleys, even pickup trucks. It is there where the church invites us to go, stretching ourselves, allowing us to feel uncomfortable, and, finally, to meet Christ.

We don't always like it, but we know we need it—instability.

FOR FURTHER DISCUSSION AND REFLECTION

How has Jesus upset your desire for a calm and secure life?

Whom do you have a hard time picturing as belonging to the church? In what ways is this a reflection of you more than of them?

20

MERCY

The Visit. It happens, at best, once a year. My dad visits from out of town. I tell my wife not to, but she always insists on rolling out the red carpet for him. The house is never cleaner. The food is never tastier. The hospitality is never grander. And the stress is never greater. (We're still recovering from the most recent visit.) I blame her, though. She's the one who told me to contact him after the birth of our first child some sixteen years ago.

As hard as I try, I can't separate the "Visit," whatever good memories result, from the "Affair," the effects of which have lingered for decades. I remember it like it was yesterday. My mom had come to pick me up from college for the holidays. Things had been strained between my parents for some time, but I was unprepared for what she would say. Breaking through the small talk, with pained eyes and faltering voice, she said, "Your father's having an affair. He's moved in with another woman."

Having had some years to mull all this over, three things help me live the very real human tension between the desire for justice and the call to mercy: two movie scenes and a

Scripture story. The first comes from the Western *Unforgiven*. In it, the outlaw, killer, turned bounty hunter Will Munny, played by Clint Eastwood, counsels the Schofield Kid after his first kill. Munny says, "It's a hell of a thing, killing a man…." To which the Schofield Kid replies, "Yeah, well, I guess they had it coming." Without missing a beat, Munny responds, "We all got it coming, kid." If justice is ultimate, we're all (not just my dad) in big trouble.

The second one involves the film *Dead Man Walking*. The movie chronicles the life-changing ministry of Sister Helen Prejean to death row inmates. Frustrated at Sr. Helen's compassionate care to the murderer of their daughter, the slain girl's parents ask why. Sr. Helen says, "I'm just trying to follow the example of Jesus who said that every person is worth more than their worst act."

I don't know about you and your lingering hurts, but for me, it's almost impossible to think of my dad and not think the worst.

Which brings me to the Story. It's one we know well: "A man had two sons, and the younger son said to his father, 'Father, give me the share of your estate that should come to me.' So the father divided the property between them" (Luke 15:11–31). The problem of the Story is that I identify with the wrong person—the elder son.

My father has long played the role of the wayward son. He left my brothers, mother, and me adrift, wondering when he was returning home. I, on the other hand, turned judgmental and jealous. Like the elder son, I was dutiful. Inwardly, though, I was a sinner consumed with envy and bitterness at the joyous reception that accompanied my father's return to relationship with others—brothers, sons, friends, and even, to some extent, the church.

In his book *The Return of the Prodigal Son*, Henri Nouwen, one of the great spiritual writers of our time, recounts a visit from a friend during which they discussed Rembrandt's painting of this parable. During the conversation Nouwen's friend said to him: "Whether you are the younger son or the elder son, you have to realize that you are called to become the father." I'm working on it.

Pope Saint John Paul II voiced much the same thing in one of his first encyclicals, Rich in Mercy (*Dives in Misericordia*): "The parable of the prodigal son expresses in a simple but profound way the reality of conversion. Conversion is the most concrete expression of the working of love and of the presence of mercy in the human world." In it Jesus is also beautifully imaged as the "Incarnation of mercy"—loving compassionately, fearlessly, totally, unconditionally, and wholeheartedly.

FOR FURTHER DISCUSSION AND REFLECTION

Referring to the characters in the parable of the prodigal son, which one is most like you? Why?

Whom do you need to picture "as worth more than their worst act"?

21

SOCIAL JUSTICE (AND CATHOLIC SOCIAL TEACHING)

If the Catholic tradition is known for anything, it's the truth (always rooted in the person of Jesus the Christ) that it proclaims. Some truths, necessarily, are more foundational than others. For example, perhaps the central theological truth Catholics believe in is a triune God—Father, Son, and Holy Spirit.

Similarly, an essential sacramental truth we hold is that Jesus is fully present in the Eucharist. As with any faith tradition that has truths that apply to all facets of life, though, some truths and teachings of faith, are disputed, resisted, or even denied.

Of all the truths of Catholicism, the ones that I struggle with the most are found in what is called Catholic social teaching. Echoed long before in the Hebrew Scriptures, the life of Jesus, and the writings of the church fathers and other notable saints, they are principles based on the fundamental dignity of the human person and the person's relationship to the wider society and environment. I don't doubt or dismiss these truths so much as fail to put them into practice.

Starting with the publication in 1891 of Pope Leo XIII's encyclical *Rerum Novarum* ("On Capital and Labor"), the Catholic Church began to articulate a vision of what it means for humans to be in relationship with one another. At the heart of this tradition is the belief that human life is sacred and deserving of protection from conception to natural death.

It should surprise no one that the Catholic Church is against abortion and euthanasia. What catches some people off guard, however, both inside and outside the church, is that Catholic social teaching is against certain actions in wars, capital punishment, hunger, exploitation of workers, poverty, and the like. Contrary to the thoughts of some well-known talk show commentators, social justice is at the heart of the Catholic tradition.

In an American culture that privileges the individual and personal freedom, Catholic social teaching says that we are first and foremost social beings. Whether Democrat or Republican, liberal or conservative, our arguments with one another over our rights rather than responsibilities make it difficult to hear God's question to Cain: "Where is your brother Abel?" (Genesis 4:9).

Often we respond like Cain: "I don't know. Am I my brother's keeper?" We don't need to be smarter than a fifth grader to know that the answer is "yes."

In the Catholic tradition then, the common good and personal good are not contradictory but complementary. At times, despite the references to the anti-Christ, government needs to be exercised instead of exorcised.

A nice summary of Catholic social teaching is captured in the statement—his inaugural address if you will—that began Jesus' public ministry: "The Spirit of the Lord is upon me, because he has anointed me to bring glad tidings to the poor. He has sent me to proclaim liberty to captives and recovery of sight to the blind, to let the oppressed go free, and to proclaim a year acceptable to the Lord" (Luke 4:18–19). In other words, Jesus wanted to "afflict the comfortable and comfort the afflicted."

As the church continues to make a preferential option for the poor and the marginalized, it also sees that the earth itself is being exploited and abused. We, too, need to respond to all of creation with preference and exercise stewardship on its behalf.

FOR FURTHER DISCUSSION AND REFLECTION

Reflect for a moment on Cain's reply to God.
In what ways are you your "brother's keeper"?

In what ways are you practicing and living out
Catholic social teaching?

22

SOME PRIESTS

I know you've heard them, maybe even passed them along.

Though we don't mention them in polite company, stereotypes and caricatures of priests exist: "Yes" men with little self-confidence who always spout back the party line, men who may listen to you in the beginning but in the end believe that "Father knows best," unimaginative and lifeless pastors who just go through the motions, self-centered individuals who have no idea what it's like to live in the real world. Suffice to say, given the events of the last two decades, it has become easy to be this one-sided in our assessment of our brothers.

Yet I know better. Over the course of my years, in a variety of ways and in many different contexts, I have come into contact with numerous priests who defy the above descriptions—who, in fact, prove them wrong.

As a student I met priests of great intellect who, as the saying goes, have forgotten more of the Catholic theological tradition than I'll ever even know. Truth for them is not something to be avoided but pursued. As a result, they not only teach the tradition but question it as well. This leads them to bring theology and Scripture into conversation with the concerns of the day: economics, history, politics, medicine, psychology, law, literature, and the like.

In my commitment for a more just world, I have worked with priests devoted to the poor and marginalized. We have marched together in Ft. Benning, Georgia, at the School of the Americas, protesting our nation's foreign policy, and in Washington, DC, at the March for Life, opposing our nation's legalizing of abortion. Like me, they are persons who seek to protect life in all its forms.

Desiring good liturgy, I have worshiped with priests who prayerfully mediate the presence of God through the Eucharist. While celebrating the church's liturgy and sacraments they make present the person of Christ. At their best, aware of their own weaknesses and limits, they truly become *alter Christus*— another Christ. Knowledgeable of the rhythms of the Spirit in a person's life, they are insightful spiritual directors. As confessors, they are compassionate in the face of one's admitted, sinful weaknesses. They also have a gift for proclaiming and connecting the word of God to people's lives.

Perhaps most importantly, at least for me, I have enjoyed the friendship of priests. I have had the opportunity to see them not as persons "up there" and set apart, but as companions on this journey. I have laughed and cried with them. We have been at each other's homes. Ultimately, and this is the basis of friendship, we have shared our lives with one another.

I have to admit some regret at the present unease that exists for many Catholics between priests and laity. The "us" vs. "them" attitude is doing little, if anything, to heal the wounds existing in our church today. I wish more people could have my type of experiences with a priest—where, when the people parted company, they would leave hoping to meet again soon.

FOR FURTHER DISCUSSION AND REFLECTION

Who are some priests that hold
a special place in your life? Why?

What can you do to affirm and encourage
the vocation to priesthood?

23

INTERPRETING
SCRIPTURE

Though it reached its zenith with the lead-up to the year 2000, every year someone says it: "The End of the World is coming." This time the date was May 21. The preacher's calculation was based upon years of reading the Bible, using mathematics to interpret hidden prophecies.

Thankfully, it didn't happen. A very sane scriptural response won the day instead: "But of that day and hour no one knows, neither the angels of heaven, nor the Son, but the Father alone" (Matthew 24:36). Like the Boy Scouts, when it comes to the end of the world, the Catholic tradition hedges its bets and says: "Be prepared." Your end is more likely to come before the end.

Speaking of another end, especially with all the rain that fell this spring, the Creation Museum in Northern Kentucky has constructed a park themed after Noah's Ark and the flood. With a petting zoo and zip lines, it is based on a literal reading of the Creation stories in Genesis. This brought to mind a story that I'd heard some years ago: a Sunday school teacher asked her young class how Noah spent his time in the ark. When there was no response, she asked, "Do you suppose he did a lot of fishing?"

In response, a six-year-old piped up, "What, with only two worms?"

Both of these scenarios—end-time prophecies and Noah's Ark theme parks—are quite foreign to Catholic sensibilities. It's not the way we interpret and/or "sell" Scripture. And, as a result, it's one of the things that keep me Catholic.

Rather than say, "God said it. I believe it. That settles it," Catholics reply, "That's not the half of it." Countering the centuries-old charge that Catholics don't read the Bible, scriptural reading and biblical literacy are regarded as key foundations for a Catholic's faith life today. This was stressed through the Second Vatican Council's Constitution on Divine Revelation (*Dei Verbum*).

As important as reading the Bible is, though, how we do it may be more important. When approaching the Bible, it is important to recognize that it is a collection of books written over an extended period to a diverse group of people.

One key interpretive tool when reading Scripture is to know the literary form. Creation stories of Genesis (myth) are different from Job (debate), which is different from Mark (a gospel). Knowing this goes a long way in beginning to understand what God is attempting to reveal to us through Scripture—"the Word of God in the words of humans." Ultimately, Scripture is most concerned about revealing religious truth to believers, not scientific or historical fact.

Another crucial tool is appreciating the historical context of what we're reading. This considers the practices and beliefs at the time the book was written, which are often very different from our own today. Knowing what a passage meant in the past, what the original author intended, better enables us to apply it to our lives today.

Taken together, then, these two keys help Catholics avoid the pitfall of fundamentalism or an overemphasis on the literal wording of Scripture divorced from its literary form, cultural context, and the teaching of the church community. As a result, when it comes to scriptural interpretation, Catholics share great sympathy with the old saying that "It ain't those parts of the Bible that I can't understand that bother me; it is the parts that I do understand."

Interpreting the Bible contextually, critically, for spiritual development is central for Catholics.

FOR FURTHER DISCUSSION AND REFLECTION

What do you wish you knew more about with respect to the Bible?

Prepare for this Sunday's readings.
Consult a Catholic commentary that looks at the readings contextually. Share your thoughts with a friend.

24

CONSCIENCE

The Freeh Report (2012) was both direct and damning in its assessment of Penn State's response to former coach Jerry Sandusky's abuse of children: "This evidence presents an unprecedented failure of institutional integrity leading to a culture in which a football program was held in higher esteem than…the values of human decency."

After reading it through the first time, I couldn't help but reword "institutional integrity" to "institutional conscience." Conscience, as we all know, is that valuing, thinking, reflecting, judging, acting, and, ultimately, humanizing part of ourselves. If we lack one or, more importantly, have a conscience that is deficient in its formation, our humanity and others' lives are often compromised. Tragically, the president, vice president, athletic director, and head football coach of Penn State enabled a child predator to rape children for "fear of or deference to the omnipotent football program."

As the Penn State case and other economic, political, legal, and religious (our own Catholic community has been devastated and called to greater accountability and transparency by a sexual abuse crisis as well) episodes over the years illustrate so well, there is a great temptation when it comes to institutions and conscience. Ideology can trump humanity. Rather than follow Christ, who said, "Let the children come to me… for the kingdom of heaven belongs to such as these" (Matthew 19:14), we can embrace the philosophy of Caiaphas who, at the Sanhedrin trial of Jesus, said, "better for you that one man should die instead of the people, so that the whole nation may not perish" (John 11:50).

Though I've never been comfortable with the slogan WWJD ("What would Jesus do?"), I'm convinced that conscience is an encounter—a living relationship—between Jesus, the context of our lives and times, and the Catholic faith community that we are members of. Forming it, exercising it, and living it are no easy tasks in our fractured and polarized world. Yet, through conscience we express who we are as human beings made in the image and likeness of God. Sadly, such is the horror, destruction, and pain when it appears that conscience has not been followed.

Here it bears repeating the significant words and weight that the Second Vatican Council places on conscience: "In the depths of his conscience, man detects a law which he does not impose upon himself, but which holds him to obedience. Always summoning him to love good and avoid evil, the voice of conscience can when necessary speak to his heart…For man has in his heart a law written by God. To obey it is the very dignity of man; according to it he will be judged. Conscience is the most secret core and sanctuary of a man. There he is alone with God, whose voice echoes in his depths" (Pastoral Constitution on the Church in the Modern World, 16).

It is in this call to search for the truth, to obey conscience, and to listen to the voice of God that the church plays a vital and necessary role. Whether it be abortion, immigration, euthanasia, war, marriage, health care, or other issues, it is incumbent upon us not only to know *what* the church teaches but *why*. As for our desired decision, the church's teaching may be confirming, challenging, or confounding. As Catholic Christians, however, we must bring the substance of the faith into consideration and conversation with the whole of our lives. More often than not we will find the two in agreement rather than opposition.

Only then does the oft-quoted line by Blessed Cardinal John Henry Newman, make sense: "Certainly, if I am obliged to bring religion into after-dinner toasts…I shall drink—to the pope, if you please—still, to conscience first, and to the pope afterward."

FOR FURTHER DISCUSSION AND REFLECTION

When did you make a significant decision in conscience? What role did the church's teachings play in it?

25

THE EUCHARIST

Speaking to medical students, Gregory House, the drug-addicted, arrogant, impersonal, yet brilliant doctor of television fame, reveals his medical motto: "It's a basic truth of the human condition that everybody lies. The only variable is about what."

Well, honestly, whether it sets us free or not (John 8:32), sometimes we tell ourselves and others it's better not to know the truth. For example, like any foolish, soon to be middle-aged male, I'd put it off for far too long—my "annual" physical exam. Perhaps I didn't want to have confirmed what I already knew—things had to change. During my conversation with the doctor we turned to health and diet. Perhaps I was too forthcoming because what I remember hearing were two things: "You can't eat that any more" and "You can't drink that anymore."

Speaking strictly as a health-conscious Catholic, whether it be food or drink, what I know I need more of is the Eucharist. The Body and Blood of Christ are said to be "the source and summit" of our faith. In this great sacrament of love, Jesus breaks the bread so that we can be made whole. As a Catholic,

I'm convinced that the Eucharist can help repair and heal the great wounds in ourselves and the culture at large.

One thing that has led us to a state of relational brokenness is individualism. We're taught at the youngest of ages to be self-reliant and independent. Admitting weakness or vulnerability is a luxury we can't afford. Yet, as Pope Benedict once shared, "In a culture that is ever more individualistic…the Eucharist constitutes a kind of 'antidote,' which operates in the minds and hearts of believers and continually sows in them the logic of communion, of service, of sharing, in a word, the logic of the Gospel." Contra Frank Sinatra and the philosophy of "I did it my way," the Eucharist shows us the way of Jesus—ever-increasing fellowship and widening of our circles of relationship.

Frustratingly, even though we know better, it is hard to resist the allure of materialism and consumerism. Yet, as Pope Francis relates, "Whenever material things, money, worldliness, become the center of our lives, they take hold of us, they possess us; we lose our very identity as human beings." As the first commandment proclaims: "You shall have no other gods beside me" (Exodus 20:3). The Eucharist calls us out of our various idolatries. It invites us to admit our deepest hunger—for relationship with God through Christ Jesus. The Gospel of John reminds us of this when Jesus says, "He who eats my flesh and drinks my blood has eternal life, and I will raise him up at the last day" (6:54). In the process, we realize that so much of what we put value in is fleeting.

Though St. Paul said to the Galatians, "There is neither Jew nor Greek, there is neither slave nor free person, there is not male and female; for you are all one in Christ Jesus" (3:28), sexism, racism, and militarism remain. Or, in other words, power, privilege, and position. The Eucharist provides an opportunity for us to encounter one another as we truly are—sons and daughters of God. The differences and walls that we want to erect or maintain fall.

Speaking in Ireland some years ago, Pope Saint John Paul II said

> The truth of our union with Jesus Christ in the Eucharist
> is tested by whether or not we really love our fellow men
> and women; it is tested by how we treat others, especially
> our families: husbands and wives, children and parents,
> brothers and sisters. It is tested by whether or not we try to
> be reconciled with our enemies, by whether or not we forgive
> those who hurt us or offend us. It is tested by whether we
> practice in life what our faith teaches us. We must always
> remember what Jesus said. "You are my friends if you do what
> I command you" (John 15:14). The Eucharist helps love to
> triumph in us—love over hatred, zeal over indifference.

FOR FURTHER DISCUSSION AND REFLECTION

*How does reception of the Eucharist build
a deeper relationship with Jesus? How does it bring
us into deeper relationship with others?*

*Echoing the words of Pope Benedict,
in addition to "antidote," what other image would
you use to describe the Eucharist?*

26

FESTIVALS

Wanting to test my hypothesis, I asked my wife what word came to her mind after "St. Rita's." Without missing a beat, she replied, "festival."

Was there any other possibility? Yes, but not really.

I knew that St. Rita's was a school for deaf children right outside Cincinnati before even asking the question. But the importance of its festival cannot be underestimated. What may surprise you is that I say this theologically, not financially.

Most Cincinnati cradle Catholics take church festivals for granted. In fact, they're synonymous with summer. They're a holy weekend of obligation, if you will. For someone like me who grew up on the northern edge of the Bible Belt in Lexington, Kentucky, however, they were a very new and appealing experience. With funnel cakes, snow cones, cotton candy, bid-n-buy, carnival rides, poker, and blackjack, it's like the state fair and Jesus combined. Who would have thought being Catholic could be this much fun?

My wife and I even had one of our first dates at a festival—

St. Cecilia's. Over the years I have become convinced that festivals—or better said the very notion of "festivity"—are one of the best things about Catholicism.

Though I don't agree with them, I can sympathize with those who say that in having festivals the church is being hypocritical and/or sacrilegious. Just look at all the drinking and gambling going on. Being guilty of these activities myself every now and then, thankfully I can count as no less a model than Jesus himself who was accused from time to time of being a "glutton and drunkard" (Luke 7:34). (One of the few times I can count myself in such good company.) It should never be forgotten that Jesus' first miracle was at a wedding in Cana (John 2:1–11). There, much to the surprise of those gathered and to the delight of the host, he turned water into wine.

I remember well the engagement party of my older brother. He was marrying a Southern Baptist. One of the first of many marital concessions was that her family allowed wine but nothing else.

The beauty of Catholicism, though, is that we're a tradition that combines both Mardi Gras (celebration) and Ash Wednesday (penance). The path to holiness comes in many shapes and forms. Jesus never separated the body from the soul, life from spirituality. Through festivals, the church takes the things of life—food, water, entertainment, family, friends, weather—and consecrates them, makes them holy or recognizes the presence of God already there. It's what the Incarnation is all about.

It is strange, then, that a common critique of Christians is that we are an angry, unfriendly, unhappy group of people. Or that what a noted American satirist and cultural critic once said of Puritans—"Puritanism: The haunting fear that someone, somewhere, may be happy"—could be said of some present-day Catholics. In the midst of her conversion to Catholicism, a woman once mused, "You say you have the truth. Well, the truth should set you free, give you joy. Can I see your freedom? Can I feel your joy?"

A rabbinic saying captures this sentiment in similar fashion: "At Judgment Day we will be called to answer for all the good things we might have enjoyed but did not."

Our reply as Catholics should be, "Get thee to a festival."

FOR FURTHER DISCUSSION AND REFLECTION

*In what ways does Catholicism bring joy
and "festivity" to your life?*

*Is it easy or difficult for you to picture Jesus laughing
and celebrating in the company of others?*

27

ACCESSIBILITY

One of the more endearing hallmarks of Pope Francis' pontificate is his desire to reach out to the faithful in a way that could be characterized as both spontaneous and familiar.

This is well illustrated in his ongoing practice of celebrating morning Masses, not in the more private setting of his official residence at the Apostolic Palace, but in the chapel at the Casa Santa Marta, the Vatican guesthouse where he has stayed since his election as pope. Here each morning, before a crowd of about fifty people, Pope Francis offers unscripted, or "off-the-cuff," homilies.

A recent one caught my attention.

In it, Pope Francis referred to an *eighth* sacrament. Many people, he said, approach parishes (and the church at large) today—for example a boyfriend and girlfriend who wish to marry or an unwed mother who asks for her child to be baptized—and find closed doors. The need to follow proper procedure, have enough money, and possess the right certificates seems to have trumped and dampened the faith of those who desire continued Christian commitment.

"We are many times controllers of faith," Pope Francis admitted, "instead of becoming facilitators…And there is always a temptation to try and take possession of the Lord. And so when we are on this road, have this attitude, we do not do good to people, the People of God." He went on to say that "Jesus instituted the seven sacraments with the attitude of an open door and we are establishing the eighth: the sacrament of pastoral customs!…Jesus is indignant when he sees these things because those who suffer are his faithful people, the people that he loves so much."

Simply put, Pope Francis prays that the church take the risk and receive the grace of greater accessibility. This is also what keeps me Catholic.

Truth be told, it's what we all yearn for—a place, a community, a people who are approachable, available, and supportive of one another. St. Paul, one of the early church's heroic missionary figures, described this hoped-for reality when he said that in the church "there is neither Jew nor Greek, there is neither slave nor free person, there is not male and female; for you are all one in Christ Jesus" (Galatians 3:28).

The word "catholic" itself challenges us to become an ever more accessible faith community. Coming from the Greek, it translates as "universal" and "inclusive." Yet, as evidenced by Pope Francis' words, far too many people, both inside and outside the church, experience it as condemnatory, fearful, elitist—a closed door.

This is where the example of Jesus is so important. In his public ministry, he overcame long-standing cultural prejudices and simmering ethnic tensions to present a God who is first and foremost love. Through his physical healings, Jesus brought people who had been cast off into the margins of society back into the fullness of community; he gave them access once again to the fullness of their humanity. In the process, Jesus came to personify the all-accessible love of God.

The challenge remains, however. How can we become a community marked by the trait of ever-increasing accessibility? What changes are being asked of us? What fears are paralyzing us? What gifts are going unrealized?

FOR FURTHER DISCUSSION AND REFLECTION

How do you make the church more accessible,
more inviting, more communal for others?

28

THE BODY

Trust me. Today it's a humbling experience.

There once was a time though when I looked forward to getting my hair cut. How could you have not—what with the Kiwanis Club gumball and fruit-flavored candy machines waiting for you there? You could never have enough loose change. I also knew that if I didn't give the barber too much trouble I was assured of a sucker at the end.

How times have changed. Yes, as I survey the floor from up high in my barber's chair, I still see hair on the floor. Just gray ones. Lots of them. Also, if the barber turns me just right, I can even catch my ever-increasing bald spot in the mirror. This, of course, reminds me about my receding hair line.

At least it keeps me honest: I'm getting old. Though I don't want to admit it, my body is not what it used to be. Yet a consoling and challenging Christian truth is that the body—physically and metaphorically—is intimately tied up in my hoped-for redemption.

Unlike other religious traditions that elevate the spiritual at

the expense of the material, Catholicism sees the two as insepa-
rably linked. We are both body and soul, integrally connected.
This is confirmed in the great "bodily" truth of Christianity—
the Incarnation—through which the Son of God "became flesh
and dwelt among us" (John 1:14).

This truth wasn't always affirmed, however. One of the
first heresies that the early church faced was Gnosticism.
The Gnostics believed that the spiritual part of ourselves was
trapped in the body, the material. The goal of life was to free
oneself, escape from the shell of the body, which was corrupt,
through knowledge of one's spiritual nature. Countering this
dualistic division of the human person, the Book of Genesis
proclaims that all of creation is good, most especially humans,
who are made in the image and likeness of God (Genesis 1:31).

Today, the church tries to chart a middle course between our
culture's idolization of the body and an unhealthy self-denial
of worldly pleasures. Yes, take pride in your physical health and
appearance, but remember there's more to life and who you are
than what you see in the mirror on the wall. Yes, renunciation
of the body and material goods is valuable but only so far as
they express gratitude for what we already have and connect us
with those whose lives are marked by suffering and injustice.

In coming to a true understanding of the body, the church,
also known as the body of Christ, looks to the person of Jesus
and the themes of brokenness and transformation. By Jesus' life
and his death on the cross, we are reminded that, though our
bodies may be places of grace, they are also ones of sin. Humanity
is broken. Out of greed and jealousy, we treat one another inhu-
manely. Instead of building each other up, we tear one another
down. Ultimately, this reaches its end in death and physical decay.

Rather than wallow in despair and fear, though, the church invites us to eternal transformation. As it was for Jesus, it is for us: death does not have the final say. Bodily resurrection awaits. What once was dead can rise anew. The bridge that anticipates this faith experience for us is the Eucharist. During its celebration, we participate in the Paschal Mystery. Through it, the bodily brokenness and sinfulness of life is admitted, yet through grace new life and friendship in Christ is foreseen and offered.

FOR FURTHER DISCUSSION AND REFLECTION

According to the Catholic tradition, the body—creation and nature—is a place where we can meet God. Do you believe this truth? Do you live it?

As part of the body of Christ, how have you experienced both the brokenness and graced reality of the church?

29

WE'RE ALL SINNERS

One of these days I'm going to write it: The Great American Novel. The book that speaks to the depth (or lack thereof) of America's soul. Who knows what it will be like to see my name mentioned alongside the likes of Herman Melville and *Moby Dick*, F. Scott Fitzgerald and *The Great Gatsby*, and Harper Lee and *To Kill a Mockingbird*.

I'm sure you've already added another author and book to my list.

Mindful of the phrase "Where angels fear to tread fools rush in," if I had to pick just one great American novel, my choice would be Nathaniel Hawthorne's *The Scarlet Letter*. Though set in seventeenth-century Puritan America, the story has much to say about our times as well through the themes of guilt, sin, mercy, condemnation, and redemption.

In the center stands the figure of Hester Prynne. Everywhere she goes she is marked by the sign of her fallen state—a scarlet "A" sown onto her clothing. Often with Hester is the fruit of her sexual indiscretion, her paradoxically named daughter, Pearl.

Her lover, the Reverend Arthur Dimmesdale, is publicly seen as a good and holy man by the townspeople. Behind closed doors, however, he is literally tortured by his guilt of leaving Hester and Pearl to fend for themselves in broad daylight. Though spiritually paralyzed to do so, Dimmesdale longs to live the truth *The Scarlet Letter*'s narrator offers at the end of the book: "Be true! Be true! Be true! Show freely to the world, if not your worst, yet some trait whereby the worst may be inferred."

The third figure in this tangled triangle of humanity is Hester's forlorn and estranged husband, Roger Chillingworth. His last name symbolically represents how his desire for revenge turns him cold to relationship. He has become what he hates.

Ultimately, the great truth, however much we deny or can't see it, is that we all wear the letter "A." Having taken in all the whispered judgments and condemning glances of her so-called Christian neighbors, Hester lives out a hard-won compassion for all. Freed from the concern of public respectability and its associated condition of self-righteousness, Hester's mark of shame becomes a badge of honor.

By the end, Hester's "A" has changed from "adultery" to "able": Able to own her contradictions. Able to become more sensitive to people's hidden vulnerabilities. Able to be more human. Able to admit that she is a sinner in need of a savior.

For some years now, after a class presentation on the book, I pass out red "A"s to all my students. I invite them, as I visibly model my own sinful state, to place this marker of the human condition in their school ID holder. Most smile when they see me do it. Some actually take me up on it.

Looking back on his experience wearing the letter, one student remarked that, "I had to take time and reflect that we are all sinners. And people became uncomfortable when I was saying I was wearing this symbol of evil to show I was imperfect. Because we as a culture like to think that we are all perfect and nothing is truly wrong."

Someone else who knows and admits his sinfulness may surprise us at first: Pope Francis. In one of his first interviews as pope he was asked to describe himself. His reply: "I am a sinner. This is the most accurate definition. It is not a figure of speech, a literary genre. I am a sinner." Perhaps that is why he is such a promoter of God's mercy.

Though we may not like to admit it, we are all sinners. In saying this, we at least open ourselves up to the person and ministry of Jesus through the church. As Jesus said, "Those who are well have no need of a physician, but those who are sick; I have come not to call the righteous but sinners" (Mark 2:17).

The most important thing, though, from Pope Francis: "God is greater than sin."

Catholics celebrate this truth in the sacrament of reconciliation. Embraced by the mercy of God in Christ Jesus, love triumphs. All we need to do is accept it.

FOR FURTHER DISCUSSION AND REFLECTION

How do you feel when you admit to yourself that you're a sinner?

How do you feel when you accept and receive the mercy of God in the sacrament of reconciliation?

30

THE CATHOLIC IMAGINATION

There's a common phrase in presidential politics—"It's the *economy*, stupid." When asked why I stay in the church I'm often tempted to reply, "It's the *imagination*, stupid."

Since my birth, in ways both conscious and unconscious, the church has provided me with numerous images, metaphors, and stories—a way to see the world. Priest, sociologist, and writer Father Andrew Greeley makes this clear in his book *The Catholic Imagination*. He writes that "Catholics live in an enchanted world, a world of statues and holy water, stained glass and votive candles, saints and religious medals, rosary beads and holy pictures." These have given me a Catholic "vocabulary" of faith that has helped me navigate the turbulent waters that make up the river of life. It's a language more hopeful than despairing, more life-affirming than world-denying.

To offer a recent example as evidence, consider the movie *Gran Torino*, starring Clint Eastwood. I will not spoil it for you when I say that you can see Eastwood's character, Walt

Kowalski, one of two ways: either as a racist, angry, disgruntled Korean War veteran, best captured in his line, "Get off my lawn," or as a Christ figure. Blame it on my Catholic imagination, but I see him as a Christ figure.

A while back I was asked to serve on jury duty. Just my luck, I was chosen as the alternate. This meant that I had to sit through all of the proceedings, but unless one of the other jurors couldn't fulfill their obligation, I would be dismissed when they went into deliberation. This is exactly how it played out.

I later expressed my frustration to my brother, who is a lawyer, and an ex-Catholic. I told him that I wanted to tell the judge that both persons were guilty and innocent at the same time. The environments they both grew up and lived in were not helpful, or hopeful, to their flourishing as human beings. His summary of the situation was a bit different from mine: "It's the fallen nature, the utter depravity of man." No Christ figures in the courtroom for him that day.

How I need the Catholic teaching that the human person is fallen but redeemable—begun through God's gift of grace, divine friendship, and followed by our response to it.

In addition to the Catholic imagination, what my brother needs is a healthy dose of the sacramental and incarnational worldview. The Catholic principle of sacramentality stresses that the divine, the unnamed and unknowable mystery, is made visible and real to us in and through the material. The infinite is experienced in the finite. Bread, wine, water, physical gestures, art, and still others, can and do lead us to the sacred. Is it any wonder, then, that Catholics love to have things blessed—food, animals, homes, religious imagery, boats, work equipment, and athletic fields?

Likewise, an incarnational way of viewing the world presents God as one who doesn't flee from the world, but, in ways we have yet to fully understand, "takes flesh" in this world. In Christ Jesus, God embraces the human condition up to and including death on a cross. The supposed innocent Nativity scenes are part of it as well. Contained within is a view of God that would change the world if we only let it. As the French Jesuit Pierre Teilhard De Chardin said, "By virtue of the Creation and, still more, of the Incarnation, nothing here below is profane for those who know how to see."

FOR FURTHER DISCUSSION AND REFLECTION

How does the Catholic tradition shape your world— what you say, what you hear, how you see, why you do things?

In looking at the spaces you inhabit, how do they reflect your Catholic worldview through images and objects?

31

JESUS IS NOT
MY PERSONAL LORD
AND SAVIOR

After a long day of teaching, I returned home to an unexpectedly quiet house. This was surprising, given our three kids were home with a babysitter. A little alarmed, I looked around the house. Nearby, I found two of our kids and the babysitter huddled under an end table in the corner of the family room.

"What are you doing?" I cautiously asked my oldest daughter, Cara. She quietly responded, "Shhh. We're playing Sardines." Just about this time, I heard my youngest daughter, Nora, calling from another room, "Where are you? Here I come."

For those of you who don't know, Sardines is the opposite of Hide-and-Seek. One person hides. Then everyone goes looking for her. When someone finds her, rather than shout out, "I see you," they join the person in their hiding spot. Eventually, just like with my kids, there is a group scrunched together, talking and giggling, trying not to give up their location. Usually, it ends in a burst of laughter when the final person finds the group that's been waiting to be discovered all along.

What a beautiful description of Catholicism. Though individual players are needed, when all is said and done, it's one big communal celebration. Everyone's safe and sound. This is what keeps me Catholic.

It has long been said by commentators on the American scene that we rebel against those who try to impose any system on us. We prize our freedoms, our choices, our individuality. It's the American way. This is true not only politically but also religiously. We like to be our own authorities—no intermediaries needed or wanted.

Sociologist Robert Bellah noted this some years ago in his book *Habits of the Heart.* He symbolized the American cultural emphasis toward religious individualism in the person of Sheila Larson. Describing her faith journey, she said, "I can't remember the last time I went to church. My faith has carried me a long way. It's Sheilaism. Just my own little voice."

This line of thinking allows countless people, separate from any support of tradition, Scripture, creed or community, to claim that "Jesus is my personal Lord and Savior."

The Catholic way, however, privileges the communal. This corresponds to the human condition as well. We are social beings, living in a culture that is scared to death of being dependent on others, yet members of a faith tradition that says there is no other way.

The operative faith pronoun is not "I," then, but "we." When it comes to our faith, for better and for worse (the two are inseparable), it has not been our own creation. We were led to and are sustained in our belief in and relationship with Jesus by others—a pilgrim community called church. On some days, it means taking one step forward; on others, it means going two steps back.

As a member of it, we can rightfully and creedally say, "For us and for our salvation he came down from heaven." Jesus didn't die for "me." God's salvific plan made manifest in the person of Jesus is to save all of creation. We are but a small part of it.

It is only with the support of a faith community that we can say, "Jesus is our personal Lord and Savior."

FOR FURTHER DISCUSSION AND REFLECTION

Where do you find, create, sustain, and celebrate community in the Catholic Church?

32

THE NATIVITY

Given the time of year, you may have already put it away. As for me, I have a hard time even getting it out—the Nativity scene.

Truth be told, it scares me.

Ever since I was a young kid, I dreaded going to church during the Advent and Christmas seasons. In front of the main altar, our parish placed a large Nativity scene. You couldn't miss it.

Depending on how close it was to Christmas, various persons began to appear—shepherds, wise men, Mary and Joseph—making their way to Bethlehem. After Mass, instead of allowing my two older brothers and me to hurry home, Mom had other ideas.

Desiring that we get more in touch with the season, she would tell us to go up to the Nativity scene and say a few prayers. So each Sunday, up we went. *Slowly.* Hoping mom would change her mind. *Grudgingly.* Offering whimpers of resistance along the way. *Uncomfortably.* With hands in pockets and heads down. *Embarrassed.* Thinking all the time that everyone was looking at us and mocking our childhood piety.

Reaching the Nativity scene, my brothers and I would kneel, say a few quick prayers, and hurry out of church.

I'm even more convinced today that my early childhood feelings of resistance were well placed, but for different reasons.

This past season, I saw the most honest and frightening Nativity yet. Ironically enough, it is at a place called Victory Park. I've driven by it countless times. In one of its corners a World War II tank is prominently displayed throughout the year. During the Christmas and Advent season, however, a Nativity scene is placed just feet away from this overpowering military machine. It is, to say the least, a jarring image. I don't know if it's there to protect the infant Jesus or run him over.

With the tank's turret pointed my way, the song I heard in my head was "Run for Cover," not the classic seasonal carol of "Hark the Herald Angels sing, glory to the newborn king. Peace on Earth and mercy mild, God and sinners reconciled."

With all due respect to St. Francis of Assisi, for too long the church has presented an image of the Nativity that is too tranquil, romantic, and picture perfect. If I didn't know better, looking at some of them, I could convince myself that Jesus is staying at a five-star resort instead of lying in a manger in a stable.

The actual historical context of the Nativity is far more dungy and dangerous. Displaced and homeless, Mary and Joseph are exhausted from their travels. In the shadows, behind the adoring shepherds and gift-bearing magi, a duplicitous and bloodthirsty King Herod is bent on retaining his power…up to and including murder.

This is the reality that disturbs me. It is also one that all the holiday catalogues, Christmas cards, and Nativity scenes try to sanitize. So many of us, myself included, would rather hide from this side of the story. Yet, the mystery of the Incarnation states the opposite. Our God, the God of Jesus the Christ, doesn't cover up the truth but reveals who we are, and who we're called to become, through it.

For this reason, our Catholic tradition celebrates that salvation is to be found in the midst of the tension, contradiction, and shadows of life.

FOR FURTHER DISCUSSION AND REFLECTION

Which character in the Nativity most parallels you? Why?

Does the symbol of the Nativity change knowing that lying at its heart is an infant with a price on his head, one who eventually will be crucified as an enemy of the Roman empire?

33

THE QUESTION
OF SUFFERING

That Friday, with my wife out of town and weather reports of severe storms—even possible tornadoes—to come, I hurried home from work. Having just arrived from school, my kids were hunkered down in the basement with books to read, games to play, a radio to listen to, and snacks to eat.

I went from being downstairs with them one moment to checking the TV's instant weather forecast upstairs the next. My wife called from Virginia to check on us. "We're fine," I told her. "It looks like the storm is going to pass us by." Thankfully, it did. Going out that evening for dinner, it was beautiful. The clouds, winds, and rain were gone. The sun was setting. A picture perfect evening.

The next morning was another story, however.

Opening up the newspaper, I saw pictures of utter devastation. Homes leveled. Cars tossed. Debris everywhere. I also read statements from people trying to make sense, incomplete though it was, of what appeared to be overwhelming suffering and pain. One lady remarked, "This was a piece of God's country, but it's not anymore." Another replied, "Tomorrow's not promised. It's another one of God's tests."

Yet, from afar, a sense of powerlessness came over me. What could I do miles away? I was quickly reminded of the words of Jesuit Father Jon Sobrino. In his book *Where Is God?* he says that whether it's a tornado, tsunami, earthquake, terrorist attack, or war, one of the first temptations in the face of tragedy is to turn away from it. The foundational (and Christian) response, though, is to allow ourselves to be affected by it. This is not a problem for the victims, but for us—those who hear about it via social media or read about it in newspapers. The challenge to not forget, to remain attentive to the needs of the poor, whose stories quickly become yesterday's news, follows.

In this way, Sobrino notes, catastrophes are "bearers of truth." They let us experience the strengths and weaknesses of communities. When faced with these "new" truths, we often want to conceal or dismiss them. This usually is because the catastrophe reveals the poverty, vulnerability, and defenselessness of a society. The call to solidarity, to bear another's burdens, whether in Indiana, Kentucky, Haiti, or Darfur, is too demanding.

Tragically, those who most bear the burdens of natural disasters, terror, and war are the poor. Sobrino describes them as a "crucified people." In them one notices a "primordial saintliness." In the midst of pain, stress, and loss, one witnesses acts of defending and struggling for life. In trying times, goodness emerges, more often than not anonymously.

This was captured well in what Fr. Michael Barth told his parishioners of St. Mary's Catholic Church in Kenton County,

Kentucky, after a tornado demolished their church: "Things happen and the way we handle it shows us whether we're God's children or not," he said. "The way community is coming together, it's the glory of God shining on us."

That sense of community was enlarged further for me when checks from a demolished bank in hard-hit Henryville, Indiana, over one hundred miles away, fell in our neighborhood. It convinced me that as much as suffering brings up the question of "Where is God?" It brings up, just as strongly, the question, "Where are my brothers and sisters in my time of need?"

We are a part of a religious tradition that not only asks hard questions about suffering, but is with the suffering in times of need, personifying the compassion of Jesus with direct assistance to those hurting. In the process, it reminds us that love of God is inseparable from love of neighbor.

FOR FURTHER DISCUSSION AND REFLECTION

In the face of suffering, how does the church help you turn to it rather than away from it?

When asked "Where is God?" by those suffering, what is your response?

34

CIVIC
RESPONSIBILITY

Before anyone dismissively accuses me of being blue, red, or green, I want to say two things: 1) It's a sin not to vote; and 2) the Tuesday after the first Monday in November should be a holy day of obligation (in America) celebrating the Feast of Civic Responsibility.

On the first point, it appears that I am in good (and papal) company. Speaking to the Congress of the International Union of Catholic Women's Leagues in Rome on September 11, 1947, Pope Pius XII said, "There is a heavy responsibility on everyone, man or woman, who has the right to vote, especially when the interests of religion are at stake; abstention in this case is in itself, it should be thoroughly understood, a grave and fatal sin of omission. On the contrary, to exercise, and exercise well, one's right to vote is to work effectively for the true good of the people, as loyal defenders of the cause of God and of the church."

Unfortunately, many view the political and democratic process as a graceless and barren wasteland. The potential exists, however, for the process and the act of voting itself to be real affirmations of faith, moments of prayer if you will.

As is made clearer each day, political issues are never "value free." They are full of moral and justice implications, or, put more bluntly: political issues are moral and justice issues that must bear the imprint of our civic and faith voices. A document that can guide us in this process of civic discernment is *Forming Consciences for Faithful Citizenship* issued by the United States Conference of Catholic Bishops.

In *Faithful Citizenship* the bishops note: "As Catholics, we are led to raise questions for political life other than 'Are you better off than you were two or four years ago?' Our focus is not on party affiliation, ideology, economics, or even competence and capacity to perform duties, as important as such issues are. Rather, we focus on what protects or threatens human life and dignity."

For some, one remedy to the complexity of political life is to vote according to one major issue. Single issues are rarely that, though. There is a whole host of other issues connected with the "one" that was thought to stand alone. There is no easy way out, then, from the often contradictory messages of campaigns and politicians. It is this every situation that has left many Catholics politically homeless.

What's a Catholic to do?

Ultimately, we must vote our conscience, guided, of course, by the wisdom of the church. Prayerful discernment is needed. Often this finds us choosing between the lesser of two evils. The religious absolute meets the political reality. This is especially true in a country as diverse and pluralistic as America.

It is good to remind ourselves here that people of goodwill and faith can and will disagree. Frustratingly, rather than leading to unity and conversation, political dialogue often devolves into polarization and discord. (Have you watched any television, visited websites, or listened to the radio lately?) But as St. Ignatius says in the *Spiritual Exercises*: "Let it be presupposed that every good Christian is more ready to save his neighbor's proposition than to condemn it." Or, in other words, we need to give other people's political persuasions the benefit of the doubt.

Thus, we are left with what appears to be simultaneously both contradictory and complementary—faith and politics. The challenge of balancing the two awaits us. This, the bishops say, is our "dual heritage as both faithful Catholics and American citizens."

So, whatever our political differences, we should all agree that there is no disagreement over the necessity of voting and bringing our Catholic worldview and values to our civic engagement.

FOR FURTHER DISCUSSION AND REFLECTION

How mindful are you of the moral and social justice teachings of the church when you vote?

35

IT'S SMELLY, NOISY, MESSY, AND CRAZY

In addition to the four classic marks of the church—one, holy, catholic, and apostolic, Pope Francis has offered four other traits for consideration and actualization—smelly, crazy, messy, and noisy. At first glance, for reasons of personal hygiene and social decorum, these "new" ones may surprise you. Yet, though not proclaimed every Sunday in the Creed, I think you'll agree these marks have always been with the church and are essential if it is to thrive in the future.

Shortly after his papacy began, Pope Francis celebrated Holy Week with the church. At the Holy Thursday Chrism Mass, when the sacramental oils used throughout the year are blessed, he called the church, priests in particular, to go to the margins of society. In the margins, Pope Francis said, one will encounter "suffering, bloodshed, blindness that longs for sight, and prisoners in thrall to many evil masters."

They'll also end up smelling. But, according to Pope Francis, this is a good thing. In anointing "the poor, prisoners and the sick, [those]...who are sorrowing and alone," priests and all those who enter into solidarity with the outcast will live with "the smell of the sheep." That supposed smell is really the odor of holiness all of us are asked to embrace in light of our baptism.

Speaking to a group at World Youth Day, Pope Francis offered some upending and, for all those who teach adolescents, counterintuitive advice: "Let me tell you what I hope will be the outcome of World Youth Day: I hope there will be noise....I want you to make yourselves heard in your dioceses, I want the noise to go out, I want the Church to go out onto the streets, I want us to resist everything worldly, everything static, everything comfortable, everything to do with clericalism, everything that might make us closed in on ourselves."

The first translations of the quote had Pope Francis encouraging persons "to make a mess." Either way there is a call here for Christians to be a disruptive force for good. The status quo is not the Kingdom of God and rightly needs to be questioned, challenged, and, ultimately, changed.

If that wasn't enough, Pope Francis seems to be comfortable with what most of us seek to resist—the chaos and craziness of life. Returning home to Rome from World Youth Day in Brazil, against the counsel of his advisors, Pope Francis held an impromptu press conference on the plane. One question dealt with the mob scene that ensued when his driver took a wrong turn and got stuck in traffic. This allowed literally thousands of people to rush his car, reach into it, and take pictures of him.

In response Pope Francis said, "The climate [in Rio de Janeiro] was spontaneous...I could be close to the people, greet them, embrace them, without armored cars. During the entire time, there wasn't a single incident. I realize there's always a risk of a crazy person, but having a bishop behind bulletproof glass is crazy, too. Between the two, I prefer the first kind of craziness."

All of these traits suggest a person—Jesus. In the Incarnation, God, through his Son Jesus, embraced and blessed the smells, noises, messes, and craziness of the world. Rather than avoid them as places where God's graces are not present, we're invited to go and seek them, aware that we'll discover Jesus in the process. Somewhat ironically, as well, the church will see its oneness, holiness, catholicity, and apostolicity realized.

So, who wants to remain in this smelly, noisy, messy, and crazy tradition?

FOR FURTHER DISCUSSION AND REFLECTION

*Have you ever tried to "sanitize" the faith
and or the person of Jesus?*

*When it comes to practicing your faith, how smelly,
noisy, messy, and crazy are you?*

36

THE
LITURGICAL
YEAR

As a teacher, much of my focus and attention is framed by two dates—the first and last day of the school year. In addition to that, rather than months or seasons, I divide my year into quarters and semesters.

I wouldn't call it burdensome, but it sure can be pressure-filled by deadlines, conferences, emails, grades, class preps and extracurriculars. There never seems to be enough time. If I'm not careful, things can easily begin to center around me and my daily activities at school.

Thankfully, there's another calendar I'm invited to follow—the liturgical year. Catholics believe that, in and through the Incarnation—the Son of God becoming human in the person of Jesus—time was transformed. It is how and where God reveals God's very self to us. Whatever the day, feast, or season, the liturgical year enables us to find Jesus in the past, present, and future.

Yet, especially during Advent—supposedly one of the holiest seasons—everything seems to be a blur. I'm reminded of a cartoon hanging on my classroom wall. In it, the Easter Bunny is telling a Thanksgiving turkey, dressed like Santa with a bag of presents slung over his shoulder, to "Hurry up, dude."

The pumpkins and stuffing, the recognition of gratitude in our lives, give way to colored eggs and wicker baskets. What, of course, gets left out in the process are the sacred seasons of Advent, Christmas, Lent, and Easter. That's okay, though, as long as I get that sale price at the department store.

Sadly, the commercial hype surrounding these times of the year is such that we often ask, "Is it over yet?" The birth of Jesus and, later, his resurrection become anticlimactic to say the least.

The liturgical year attempts to focus our attention on the saving events and amazing characters of our faith tradition. As Americans, we are all too ready to celebrate July 4 and Presidents' Day. As disciples, shouldn't this be even more the case with the birth, life, death, resurrection, and ascension of Jesus?

In a culture of instant gratification and constant distraction, this awareness of and attention to spiritual matters is difficult to sustain. Still, the church offers us the antidotes of Advent, Lent, and Ordinary Time. Through them, we learn that patience is not only a virtue, but life. There is no banquet without first planting the seeds of the harvest.

Over the course of time—over the liturgical year—we admit that though we may be further along than in the beginning, we're still not where we need to be. The pilgrimage of faith continues. One of the prefaces for the Eucharistic Prayer captures well the rhythm and mystery of the liturgical year when it proclaims: "By his birth [Christ] brought renewal to humanity's fallen state, and by his suffering, canceled out our sins; by his rising from the dead he has opened the way to eternal life, and by ascending to you, O Father, he has unlocked the gates of heaven."

It cannot be overstated that to experience the strength and fullness of the liturgical year, one needs to be a participating member of a practicing and witnessing faith community. It is what allows us to distinguish between Black Friday, that high holiday of consumerism, and Good Friday, the day that begins death's transformation into eternal life.

FOR FURTHER DISCUSSION AND REFLECTION

What do you do to stay mindful of the liturgical year so that you don't fall into the endless routine of life?

How do Advent and Lent shape your celebrations of Christmas and Easter?

37

TRADITION
AND CHANGE

The headline made me stop my internet surfing: "World's Oldest Priest." Intrigued, I clicked on the link.

Accompanied by pictures, the article noted that Father Jacques Clemens had just celebrated his one hundred fifth birthday. Some thirty years after his official retirement, Father Clemens still holds a regular service each day at St. Beloit Church in Nalinnes, Belgium.

Reading the story, I thought to myself, "If anyone has ever lived the fullness of the Catholic tradition alongside some of twentieth century's major cultural, political, and religious events, it would have to be he."

Around the same time, I came across another article. In it a pastor from New Hampshire spoke of the difficulty of closing and consolidating parishes. He said, "It makes it a little more painful because you always expect your church and your faith community not to change."

In the midst of life's upheavals and instability—whether familial, spiritual, or national—it's hard to keep a healthy sense of balance between continuity and change. So much appears at stake. Relationships are strained. Hearts are pulled. Judgments are conflicted. Nothing illustrates these tensions better than the musical *Fiddler on the Roof*.

Set in the waning years of Czarist Russia, Anatevka is a village seemingly untouched by modern times. For Tevye, however, this traditional world will soon be upset by the marriages of his five daughters and an imperial decree evicting him and his fellow Jewish neighbors from their homes.

In the beginning, Tevye explains the image of the musical's title: "A fiddler on the roof. Sounds crazy, no? But in our little village of Anatevka, you might say every one of us is a fiddler on the roof trying to scratch out a pleasant, simple tune without breaking his neck. It isn't easy. You may ask, 'Why do we stay up there if it's so dangerous?' Well, we stay because Anatevka is our home. And how do we keep our balance? That I can tell you in one word: tradition!…Without our traditions our life would be as shaky as, as…as a fiddler on the roof!"

But what actually is this word that we hear so frequently? It comes from the Latin *traditio*, which means to "hand on." Most of the time, we speak of tradition as content or a thing—teachings and practices passed down through successive generations of believers. The challenge, then, becomes determining which ones are essential ("T") and can't be changed and which ones are customs and therefore more open to possible reform ("t").

Determining this isn't as easy as you'd think. Father Michael Himes, professor of theology at Boston College, images tradition by comparing it to a motion picture versus a photograph.

In an attempt to preserve Tradition, the photograph looks to freeze and, ultimately, betray Tradition by limiting it to a particular place and time. The motion picture, however, sees Tradition as an ongoing process whereby, in order to stay where one has always been, movement is required. As Pope Saint John XXIII said at the Second Vatican Council, "We are not on earth to guard a museum but to cultivate a flourishing garden of life."

Necessarily, then, the cultivating of Tradition requires conversation. A saying by Jaroslav Pelikan is apt: "Tradition is the living faith of the dead; traditionalism is the dead faith of the living." In asking what is of essence to Catholicism, we have to talk with those who have gone before us in faith. At the same time, we have to be mindful of the signs of the times. This will enable us to share the faith with future generations. For Tradition to be authentic, past, present, and future must come together. In other words, we can't hold onto Tradition so tightly that we strangle it, or so loosely that it slips through our hands.

In this sense, whether we can play an instrument or admit our fear of heights, tradition enables us to be a "fiddler on the roof."

FOR FURTHER DISCUSSION AND REFLECTION

What is a tradition that you participate in? What is being communicated through it? Has it changed at all over the years?

What church tradition enables you to "converse" or connect with those who have come before you, those who are with you now, and those who will come after you in the future?

38

FREE-RANGE
SPIRITING

As a parent I don't want to be one, and as a teacher I don't want to meet one: the much maligned and caricatured "helicopter parent." Like their flying namesake, they hover. Always within reach. Inserting themselves in their children's lives to an excessive degree. Never letting them be free to succeed or fail.

Unlike my own youthful days, so much of life for children today is planned with little left to possible error, chance, or imagination; too much "programming." Creativity is out, while structure is in. And yes, I've been guilty of this.

Some recent studies have shown, however, that this desire to help our children avoid negative experiences actually may be harming them. Research seems to indicate that the more parents interfere in making choices for their children the less satisfied they feel. This parental over-involvement appears to lessen a sense of autonomy, leaving children more dependent and less accountable.

The church, too, can and has played the role of the helicopter parent. As one theologian commented, "It often places more value on the bureaucratic apparatus in the church than in the enthusiasm of the Spirit; it often loves the calm more than the storm, the old which has proved itself more than the new which is bold." And, in all honesty, who can blame it? As a parent I too appreciate order, peace and quiet, and the tried and true. It's safer, saner, and makes me, to say nothing of my children, feel more secure.

Yet in the face of all this, some argue that what is needed is "free-range parenting." Mindful of possible risks, these parents seek to instill in their children a sense of judgment that comes with experience that will enable them to become responsible adults. For this to happen freedom is required. Maturity is the desired result. Pain and suffering are always possible.

For me, the Pentecost event is a moment whereby the church lived out the tension between "helicopter" and what I now call "free-range spiriting." Gathered in the Upper Room, the disciples struggled to deal with the death of their master—Jesus. Just days before, they had hoped of God's kingdom breaking forth in their midst. Now there was real fear for their lives in light of Jesus' crucifixion. Behind locked doors (John 20:19) they took stock of what to do next.

The smart choice—disband, say they gave it their best shot, and return to their past lives. But the call and invitation of discipleship offered another possibility—enter into the grace and mystery of the Spirit.

Speaking to a group of recently installed bishops, Pope Francis encouraged them to let the Spirit "continually turn your life upside down." I'm sure they were surprised to hear this being part of their job description. Here the pope was telling them "not to tame such power."

Whether it is the early church or us today, this confused and fearful community of faith has had the Spirit breathed upon it. Complacency and comfort are, therefore, not its lot. Like Jesus, we have been anointed, empowered, and guided by the Spirit to bring forth God's presence to a world sorely in need of it.

If only we had more trust in the Spirit's transforming presence. When troubles come, something inside tells us to play it safe. Yet the creative, life-giving Spirit beckons us to go beyond our limited horizons, to challenge unjust structures, and to live in the Kingdom that we are promised in faith.

FOR FURTHER DISCUSSION AND REFLECTION

When have you, despite fears, let the Spirit guide you?
What happened? Where did you end up?

Is there anything the church needs to change or let go of so that the Spirit can be more present in the lives of believers?

39

HELL'S
JUDGMENT

Perhaps it was just a coincidence, but as summer's span of days over ninety degrees continued, my thoughts turned to hell.

There I was cutting the yard of a neighbor. Witnessing my sweat-drenched shirt and wilting frame, she kindly brought me out a glass of water. In the midst of my hydration break, we got to talking about financial matters. At one point, we touched upon how beneficial endowments can be to an organization's stability.

It was then she told me a story about how her own Unitarian Universalist church was establishing an endowment for its financial security and future. Longtime members of the community were ready to donate to it. Before they did, however, they received an invitation to an estate planning meeting (free lunch included), which they gladly attended. Unfortunately, after putting their retirement savings in the hands of a supposedly well-educated individual with expert knowledge in retiree issues, their money went down the drain in a Ponzi scheme.

As someone who is increasingly nearing the downside of life expectancy, I find it unbelievable, though I know it happens, that people exploit the elderly. Knowing that I still had to trim her yard, I told her, "I hope there's a place in hell for people who do stuff like that." Handing her back her empty glass of water, I laughingly added, "That's why I'm not a Unitarian Universalist" (many of whom believe that everyone will be saved).

Some years ago, a book entitled *Whatever Became of Sin?* by Karl Menninger captured many people's interest. Though sin still exists, the book argued that we no longer name it as such. We've rationalized ("I was under a lot of pressure then") or psychologized ("I was an emotional wreck at the time") it away, avoiding any personal responsibility.

As evidenced in the popular book *Love Wins* by Rob Bell, today you could do much the same with a book entitled *Whatever Became of Hell?* Emphasizing God's all-loving character, many people say "Hell doesn't exist." Or, even if it does, God would never send anyone there because, well, God is love.

Yet, as uncomfortable or embarrassed as it makes us, the church has not done away with the teaching of hell. It still exists. Moving beyond a geographic location of molten lava and red, goat-faced, pitchfork-carrying creatures, however, some see hell as a condition or state. In this sense, hell, or eternal punishment, isn't something that God does to us, but that we do to ourselves.

Made for relationship with God and others, we can exclusively focus on the self. Loneliness, frustration, and alienation are usually the result. God is still reaching out to us; we're just refusing the invitation to God's grace and friendship. As Pope Saint John Paul II said, "Hell indicates the state of those who freely and definitively separate themselves from God." Now, erring on the side of salvific hope, to the church's credit, it has never officially said that any specific person is in hell.

In the meantime, having had some time to think about my earlier damning comment about the swindler, I have found myself to be a judgmental jerk. I've come to the conclusion that picturing other people in hell makes me feel better, though I don't think it actually makes me better.

As Pope Francis said in one of his weekly audiences in St. Peter's Square: "Whoever believes themselves just and judges others and scorns them is corrupt and a hypocrite. Arrogance compromises every good action, empties prayer, distances from God and others." The comments, taken from the parable of the Pharisee and the tax collector (Luke 18:9–14), serve as a reminder that our prayer should be for the salvation of all, such that hell is empty.

FOR FURTHER DISCUSSION AND REFLECTION

Have you ever damned someone to hell?
What were the circumstances?

Whom are you praying for such that they will
avoid hell and enter into heaven?

40

EPILOGUE:
PRACTICE, PRACTICE,
PRACTICE

Though it's a story that has made the rounds, it still speaks a great truth. As it's told, a tourist to New York City gets off the subway and heads up to the street. There, in an attempt to get his bearings straight and anxious about getting to his concert on time, he says to a New Yorker, "Excuse me, sir, but how do I get to Carnegie Hall?"

Without missing a beat, the New Yorker responds, "Practice, practice, practice."

On several levels, it wasn't what the tourist wanted to hear. But it's true.

If only things came easily. But, if life is about anything, it's practice. Unfortunately, living in a culture of instant and self-gratification, practice is a concept that has fallen on hard times.

Watching my son play basketball over the years, I've uttered to myself on more than one occasion, "How did he miss that breakaway layup?" The answer is pretty clear, though the remedy is a little more time-consuming. It takes practice to run down the court with basketball in hand, dribbling under control, defenders on your heels, and put the ball in the hoop.

Likewise, one of my daughters is a budding dancer. From time to time I have seen her look with envy at some of the older dancers who are able to do splits with what seems to be the greatest of ease. Yet, training one's body, stretching the muscles, and rehearsing the slow and required motions to do splits takes time…and practice.

Full disclosure: When it comes to the practice of my faith, I'm not that good a Catholic. All you have to do is look at me on Ash Wednesday. I have ashes on my forehead. A lot of them. I get a little nervous when I hear the person giving me the ashes say, "Repent, and believe in the Gospel." It is the ring of truth resounding in my ears.

Later it always hits me. What keeps me Catholic? One word: Ashes. Through them I admit to myself and others that I need to better practice my faith. Lent (and the other times of the year as well) is a privileged time for us fledging followers of Jesus to become better disciples of Christ.

How do we open ourselves up to God and others? Practice prayer. How do we embrace a life of simplicity and recognize the poor in our midst? Practice fasting. How do we admit the blessing that is our life and share it with others? Practice almsgiving.

Over the course of forty days, Lent gives us the opportunity to practice our faith in a more intentional way. Depending on the person, it may take a variety of forms—increased Mass attendance, daily prayer, devotions like the stations of the cross, going to Friday fish frys, celebrating the sacrament of reconciliation, and the like.

As Catholics we're rightly concerned about practice. In fact, we have names for those who supposedly don't: Chreasters (Christmas and Easter), A&P-ers (Ash Wednesday and Palm Sunday), Cultural Catholics, Lapsed Catholics; etc....Thank goodness you and I are better and truer Catholics than these groups.

Lent, however, cautions us in our self-righteous judgments. As much as we'd like to state otherwise, the season of Lent reminds us that we've all failed, all sinned, all lapsed in the practice of our faith. It is humbling realization indeed.

Our Lenten, lifelong, Catholic resolution, then? Practice, practice, practice.

FOR FURTHER DISCUSSION AND REFLECTION

What practices keep you Catholic? How often do you do them—daily, weekly, monthly, yearly?

What is one practice of Catholicism that you should consider taking up? Why?